TOP JOB SEARCH STRA

Employment opportunities will be plentiful in 2017, but if you want to find a really good job this year, you're going to need a plan....

TOP JOB SEARCH STRATEGIES FOR 2017

By DON ALLEN

Careerxpress Publishing
2017

Top Job Search Strategies For 2017

Printed in the United States of America

ISBN-13: 978-1548376406

ISBN-10: 154837640X

Table of Contents

Introduction

If you're in the market to find a new job in 2017 - or you're looking to upgrade the job you already have - you should know that the employment opportunities today are better than they've been in years. 2016 was a solid year for job growth (the best since 1999), and the trend is only expected to accelerate in 2017 and beyond. The unemployment rate is below 5% (as of Jan 2017), consumer spending is on the rise, gas prices are down, and companies both large and small are expanding their operations and hiring new workers.

And these aren't just low-paying retail or service industry jobs being created in this revitalized economy. Just about every sector of the economy is experiencing strong job growth, including manufacturing, health care, construction, government, finance, transportation, mining, information services and more.

With more people working - and gas prices lower than they've been in years – family budgets rose in 2016, and consumer confidence rose right along with it. People are spending more as a result, which benefits the U.S. economy overall. Companies are expanding their operations, and are hiring more employees to keep up with strong consumer demand. Manufacturing jobs should show strong gains this year, the health care sector will see growth fueled by the Affordable Care Act, and stronger housing demand will drive gains in construction and finance.

This Should Be a Great Year for Job-Seekers

This obviously bodes well for unemployed workers, even those who've been out of work for 18 months or longer. College graduates are expected to benefit the most in 2017, along with workers who have specialized skills in this ever-changing digital economy. This should also be a good year for currently-employed individuals who are looking to change careers, or find a better-paying job in their current field.

The stronger job market should also drive up wages for most workers, as employers are forced to pay more to attract and retain good workers. Many employees - especially recent college grads with in-demand degrees - will be able to pick and choose from multiple job offers in high-paying industries. This sort of bidding war over workers is something that was almost unheard of just a few years ago, when companies were laying off more workers than they were hiring.

This strong job growth won't be evenly distributed across the U.S., however. Some areas of the country will offer greater employment opportunities than others. For example, the oil shale boom has created thousands of high-paying jobs in places like North Dakota, while the technology sector is booming in states like Washington, Texas and California. On the other hand, some regions of the country are still experiencing double-digit unemployment rates. So if you're not willing to pack up and re-locate to where the jobs are, you might find your job search more challenging (but certainly not impossible!)

Think of Yourself as a "Free Agent" in Today's Job Market

Job seekers and career changers today can't rely on the strategies that worked twenty, ten, or even five years ago. With the explosion of social media sites like Facebook and LinkedIn, and online career resources like Monster.com, today's job search looks very different than it did just a few years ago. A recent survey indicated more than half of new employees found their job through a social media connection rather than through a headhunter or employment agency. So the ability to network and connect with prospective employers is more important than ever.

It's also important to think of yourself as a "free agent" these days, and develop a personal marketing plan that will get you the most exposure, and help you stand out from the competition in today's inter-connected job market. This means more than just having a great resume and cover letter, but also knowing how to get your resume in front of the right people, and landing those all-important interviews where you can sell yourself to the people who make the hiring decisions at your target employer.

How to Use This Book

I've organized this book into twelve sections. Each section covers a different strategy for finding a good-paying job in today's competitive and ever-changing job market. You'll learn things like how to create a job search action plan, and how to start building a personal brand that will set you apart from your competitors. There's a section on resume writing, and how to prepare for a job interview. You'll learn a variety of online job-search techniques as well, and how to use the top employment websites and blogs. I've also covered the top three social media platforms for job-seekers, and I've added some ideas for offline job searching as well.

You can read this book from cover-t0-cover, or pick out specific chapters that apply to your current situation. You may already be familiar with some of these strategies like how to use Facebook for a job search, but others may be new to you. I've attempted to provide as many useful tips as possible within each strategy, so you can learn quickly and apply that knowledge to your job search going forward.

Whatever your approach, just know that this should be a very good year for the US labor market, and your chances of finding a good-paying job are better than they've been since 2008. My intention in writing this book is to help as many people as possible take advantage of these opportunities, and hopefully find work that's both stimulating, and financially rewarding. Those jobs are out there. All you have to do is decide what you want out of a new job, create a solid plan, and then work that plan every day, with confidence. If you do those things, and you're persistent, then I have no doubt that you'll be successful in your endeavor.

Best of luck to you and THANK YOU for letting me be a part of your quest to find that exciting new job in 2017!

To your success,

Don Allen

Chapter 1: Develop a Job Search Action Plan

If you're serious about finding a great job in 2017, you'll need to have an action plan to take you from where you are now, to where you want to be. The job outlook is moving in a positive direction this year, but that doesn't mean you won't have to work hard and be determined when searching for a good-paying job in the field of your choice. There's still a lot of competition out there, and will only increase as more long-term unemployed workers re-enter the labor force now that hiring has accelerated.

Your first course of action should be to develop a comprehensive job-search plan that covers all the bases, and will put you in position to secure that ideal job when it becomes available. Many people go about the task of finding a new job in a haphazard fashion, and their results are usually less-than-ideal because of it. Sure, some people get lucky and find a great job after a few hours networking on Facebook or Twitter, but that's the exception, not the rule.

So spend the time to think things through, and formulate a plan that will get your resume out there in front of as many prospective employers as possible. And not just any employers, but hiring agents and recruiters at the companies you really want to work for.

Here are some concrete steps you can take as you develop your job-search action plan:

Step #1: Get Into the Right Mindset

Developing the proper job-search mindset means deciding right now that you're going to dedicate your full time and attention to finding that great new job in 2017. You'll be committed, focused, and unrelenting in your pursuit of that ideal position. You'll make finding that new job your full-time occupation. Many people want a new job - they think and talk and dream about it - but they never take any concrete action towards making their goal a reality. It's just empty talk. And so they wake up six months or a year later, and they're stick right where they started, with that dream job no closer to becoming a reality.

Don't be one of those people. Decide right now to pour all of your time and effort to finding meaningful work this year. Realize that in all likelihood this task won't be easy, and it will require a great deal of energy, planning, perseverance, and a thick skin. For most people, the process of job-hunting is a roller-coaster of highs and lows, and can be full of rejection and frustration at times. You'll need strong beliefs, and an iron-strong commitment to keep going even when things look bleak and you're ready to give up.

Also, don't try to rush the process. If you're currently employed and have a steady paycheck coming in, you can afford to take your time and be methodical about your job search. You won't need to panic and take the first offer that comes along (unless of course it's the one you really want). Stick to your plan, remain patient, and consider all your opportunities carefully before taking a new position.

On the other hand, if you're unemployed right now, you may not have the luxury to be patient as you wait for the best job offer to come your way. If you're married, you might be able to get by on your spouse's income while you wait and carefully consider every opportunity. Another option is to find temp or part-time work while you're looking as a way of paying the bills while you wait for the ideal job to come your way.

Whatever route you choose, be aware that job-hunting is real work, and the reward you're seeking may not come easy. It's a jungle out there, as the old saying goes, and you'll need to be mentally prepared for anything that comes your way. Don't let a temporary setback or failure stop you. Adopt the mindset that you're willing to do just about anything to find that job of your dreams, and stick with it until that new job is a reality.

Step #2: Start a Career Discovery Journal

When working with a new client, I always advise them to start a career discovery journal. A journal can help clarify and focus your thoughts, and help guide you on your journey toward the work you were meant to do. There are plenty of electronic devices capable of recording and storing your journal, but I've always preferred an old-fashioned spiral notebook for journaling. I like being able to flip through a paper notebook, jot things down, doodle, cross thing out, and even tear out pages from time to time. Plus you don't have to worry about losing all your work if your computer crashes or you drop your tablet on the floor.

Whatever you use, just know that a journal can be a great career discovery tool. The process of writing down your thoughts can be enlightening and empowering, and often leads you in directions you might not have even considered when you began your journal. Think of this as a sort of free-association exercise, turn off your internal editor, and let your thoughts flow as you scribble and draw and fill your journal with anything that pops into your head.

Keep in mind that there are no right or wrong answers in this process, and you won't be graded on what you write in your journal. Like a diary, this is for your eyes, and your eyes only. Nothing is too outlandish or off limits here. Allow yourself the freedom to imagine anything in your life, regardless of how ridiculous or impossible it may seem. You can always go back and cross things out later as you narrow down the possibilities.

Here are some sections you could include in your journal:

- Attitudes about your current job or career
- Your talents, education & work experiences
- Your passions, interests & values
- Your personality
- Your personal vision for the future
- Some career possibilities
- Taking action & making it happen

I often go back and look at things that I've written over the years in my own career discovery journal. It's fascinating to read what I wrote down at different points in my life, and to see what my thought process was at that time. Some of my goals have been realized, some of them haven't, but I've learned something from all of my successes and failures. So start your own journal now. Sometimes just the process of putting your goals and dreams down on paper makes them real, and moves you one step closer to making them happen in your life.

Step #3: Decide Exactly What You Want From Your Next Job

This may sound obvious, but it's amazing how many people set out to find a new job or career without really know what they're looking for. They might have a vague notion of wanting to make more money, or finding work that's more interesting and rewarding, or a job that will give them more free time to spend with their family. But unfortunately, that's about as far as they get toward identifying their ideal job or career.

It's hard to hit a target you can't see, or you don't even know what it looks like. So it's time to do a little soul searching, and go through a personal self-assessment. Identify the type of work you really want to do - not just today, but well into the future - and then decide what it will take to make that job a reality.

A good starting point is to imagine the career of your dreams. If you could choose any job in the world, what would that job be? What about it would interest and excite you? Why would that job be rewarding and fulfilling in a way that your current (or previous) occupation isn't? How much money would you like to make, and what kind of benefits would you like to have in that ideal new job?

Also think back to some of the jobs you had in the past, and identify things that you really enjoyed about those jobs (hopefully you can recall at least a few positive experiences). Then open your career journal and list out all the things you enjoy doing, past and present. Not just work-related activities, but in your life as a whole. Include hobbies, volunteer experiences, job accomplishments you take pride in, co-workers you like (or liked) working with, etc. Turn off your internal editor and write down anything that comes to mind.

You might also consider taking an online personality quiz . There are a number of these available, some more involved than others. A few of these quizzes are free, but most sites charge a fee for the more extensive personality assessments. This can be a good way to "step back" and take an objective look at your personality, your likes and dislikes, and what type of work would be the best match for your individual traits.

Also take time to consider what level of income and benefits you'll be seeking from your next job. Just about everyone is looking to make more money, especially as they advance further into their career. Will your new job pay as well or better than the one you have now? Will there be a good opportunity for advancement? And if so, how far? What about the benefits? Will this new position provide health insurance, paid vacation and sick days, a retirement plan, etc.?

Take your time with this step, and make sure you know what you're looking for out of a potential new job. Otherwise you risk taking a job, only to discover that it's no better than the one you had, and you're just as unhappy as you were before. If you're currently unemployed - or you liked your previous job - this might not be an issue. But you should always try to hone in on a career that will line up with your interests, passions, and core values, and is something you'll enjoy doing over the long term.

Step #4: Determine if You Need Additional Education or Training

Now that you've identified the type of job you're looking for, the next step is to determine if you'll need any additional education or training in order to secure a position in that industry. A good place to start is by looking at some online job postings. What type of degrees, certifications, and skills are necessary for an entry-level job in your target career field? And how does that match up with your current qualifications?

If you're targeting a job similar to the one you have now, you might not need a lot of additional education or training. If you're looking to move into an entirely different career field, however, you'll probably need to go back to school and earn a degree or certificate in order to land a job - or even an interview - in that field.

There are a wide variety of educational outlets available today, including local and online colleges and trade schools, where you can attend classes full or part-time. Most of them offer financial assistance in one form or another. Some companies will even offer to pay for part of your education, as long as you agree to work for them once you've completed your requirements.

If it's on-the-job experience you need, you might consider taking a part-time job, or an apprentice or volunteer position. Not only will you gain valuable skills and insight into the job, you'll also learn first-hand the pros and cons of your future career. There's nothing like rolling up your sleeves and doing the work on a daily basis to understand what the job is all about. And as an added benefit, you'll meet a lot of people who are already working in the industry, and you'll make valuable contacts who you can add to your professional network.

Finally, don't get discouraged if your target occupation will require a lengthy degree or certification program, even if you're an older worker and you can't afford to quit your job to attend school full-time. If you're currently working, you could map out a plan for attaining that additional education over time – perhaps by taking night classes at your local community college. If you're currently out of work - and you need to find a new job quickly - you may have to put your plan for that new career on hold while you secure temporary employment. Or if you have a spouse who works, they might be able to support you while you go back to school.

Step #5: Start Researching Potential Jobs & Employers

Once you've identified what type of job you're looking for - and you've determined that you have the necessary qualifications for that new job – then it's time to start researching potential employers. Fortunately, with the reach of the Internet and social media, you'll be able to do most of your research from the comfort of home. The down side to this is the fact that you can quickly become overwhelmed by the sheer volume of information available, and become lost in a sea of employment websites, blogs, company sites, recruiter sites, job boards and more.

So it's necessary to narrow down your search as much as possible, before you start Googling names and mass-submitting your resume to dozens of employers. Make a list of things you're looking for from a potential employer. Be sure the company is hiring, and is located in your geographical area. Save yourself a lot of time and aggravation by narrowing down your choices before you begin your search, that way you'll be able to focus on firms that look like a good fit for you. You'll be spending 40 hours per week (or more) at this job, after all, so you'll want to get this right.

Once you have a short-list of potential employers, it's time to start examining those companies online. Visit each company's website, and start building a picture of who they are and how they operate. What does the company do, exactly? What are their expectations? What are their core beliefs and values? How do they treat their employees? How do they envision their organization growing into the future? What are they likely to pay a new employee, and what type of benefits do they offer? What are the prospects for advancement?

Find out as much as you can about an employer before you even consider going in for an interview. This might seem obvious, but you'd be surprised at how many people apply for a job without even visiting the company's website or Facebook page. This should be your first task, as every company displays information that they're proud of on their site, including their history, their hiring practices, growth projections, key employees, human resources, contact information, and more.

Also, don't just rely on just their website for information. If your target employer is located nearby (and they should be), then drive over to their HR department and talk to some of the people there. Introduce yourself and ask them for a brochure and any other information about their company. Ask them how they like working there, how the company treats them, and if they think the firm has a bright future.

Then compile all of this information in your journal and try to get a "big picture" view of the company, and if it would be a good fit for you. Would you enjoy working for this firm – not just today, but three or five years from now? Is there growth potential? What about the hours? Is it an easy commute, or would you grow tired of the drive after a year or two? How will your family fit into the equation?

Only after you've answered these questions (and more) should you consider submitting your resume and cover letter to that firm.

Step #6: Prepare a Well-Rounded Job-Search Strategy

Chances are, you won't find the new job you really want on the first few attempts. It's a competitive economy these days, with many job-seekers vying for the same openings. You'll need to prepare yourself for the long haul, and get used to the idea that you'll probably be applying to dozens or even hundreds of firms before you land that ideal position.

So it's important to have a solid blueprint for how you'll conduct your job search. Your blueprint should be a step-by-step action plan that will lead you from where you are now (unemployed, or unhappily employed), to where you want to be (working in your ideal job). Without a well-thought-out strategy, most job searches are unfocused and haphazard, and usually result in a new job that's less than what you wanted.

Gone are the days when you could fill out a few applications, post your resume on one or two online job boards, and you'd receive dozens of good job offers. Sure, you might get lucky with this sort of part-time, scattershot job search, but it's more likely that you'll end up feeling frustrated, angry, or disillusioned with the entire process.

Instead, you should look to develop a well-rounded job search strategy that doesn't only rely on online resources. Consider offline search methods as well, things like job fairs, employment agencies, One-Stop Career Centers, your personal network, and more. By having a well-balanced strategy you'll have access to many more opportunities, and greatly increase your chances of finding that quality job you really want.

Step #7: Finally, Keep Your Job Search Going

If you're really committed to finding that exciting new job in 2017, decide that failure isn't an option. Decide that you'll keep going in your job search, until an employer says the words "You're hired, when can you start?" To succeed in today's cutthroat labor market, you simply can't afford to take a lot of time off or "go easy" in your efforts. Doing a little bit, once in a while, isn't good enough. Give yourself a pat on the back when you send off a stack of resumes to potential employers, but don't leave it at that. Follow up on those letters, and be persistent (but not annoying) in your attempts to land that all-important job interview.

Today many companies are swamped with applications, and to cope they've lengthened the time they're allowing to fill job openings. So make sure to follow up with employers, and see if they'll provide you with a reasonable timetable as to when the position will be filled. This serves two purposes: it gives you an idea of how long you can expect to wait to hear back on the opening, plus it shows the hiring manager that you're still interested in the job. It's surprising to me how many job searchers do all of the work up front, but then neglect to follow-up on the opening they're so eager to fill.

Also, make sure your online profiles are up to date. Always be looking for opportunities to add valuable contacts to your personal network. Interact with employers on social media, and look for ways to add value and be helpful to your list of followers. Keep building your personal brand, and let people know who you are, and what you'd bring to the table as a potential employee. Keep your name circulating, even after you've found a job and your job search is over.

A job search is another one of those activities where the more you put into it, the more you'll get back (and the sooner you'll see results). Decide to invest as much time, energy, and effort as you can into your search for that ideal new job in 2017, and you should see your efforts rewarded. And don't get discouraged if you're not successful right away. Most of the best things in life don't come easy (or quickly), but they're worth pursuing nonetheless.

Chapter 2: Your Personal Marketing Plan

All right, now that you've mapped out some goals for your job search, and put a preliminary plan in place, now it's time to take things a step further by developing a personal marketing plan to go with it. As you probably know, things are competitive out there, and if you want to stand out from the crowd, it's essential to market yourself just like a big company would. Your effectiveness at promoting your unique skills and abilities to employers could well determine your success in finding that new job this year.

Job-seekers who are engaged and creative stand a better chance of success. The idea is to formulate a precise marketing plan that gets you "out there" and noticed by potential employers and recruiters in your target industry. A marketing plan can contain many things, but in this chapter we'll focus on creating a personal mission statement, a unique selling proposition, and writing a personal "elevator pitch" that you can recite at a moment's notice.

You may be wondering if all this is necessary. Creating and implementing this type of marketing plan will require effort on your part, after all, and you'll need the will to see it through. But in today's dog-eat-dog economy, you can't rely on the job search tactics that worked ten or twenty years ago. Many of the traditional methods of finding a job simply aren't as effective as they used to be. Modern technology has changed the game for job-seekers in 2017, and you need to update your job-search methods accordingly.

Today you need to think of yourself as a brand name, sort of like a new soft drink or home-improvement product that you're bringing to market. But instead of promoting your brand to consumers, you'll be marketing it to recruiters and potential employers. Being a shameless self-promoter is an essential component of this strategy, and you'll need to be aggressive in contacting and networking with as many people in your target industry as possible.

There are many benefits for job-seekers who are willing to put in the time and effort to create a personal marketing plan, and then implement that plan. Some of these include:

- You'll separate yourself from the competition. And have no doubt that the competition is out there – many others will be seeking that same great job opening that caught your eye. So make sure you have a better message than they do, and that it is broadcast louder and clearer.

- You'll build a community of followers. If your marketing plan is successful, you'll accumulate a network of people who appreciate you, and who will help promote you to others in your target industry. This sort of word-of-mouth advertising is invaluable when you're looking for a new job.

- You'll establish a level of trust. If part of your marketing plan includes building a social media presence (and it should), than this will help broadcast your brand to a large online audience. And if you're consistent with your message, and you avoid the "hard-sell" tactics, you'll establish a level of trust with the people in your social networks.

Okay, now that you're aware of some of the benefits of having a personal marketing plan, you're probably wondering how to go about creating such a plan for yourself. Here are some straightforward steps you can take to outline your personal brand, and identify your job-search objectives:

Step #1: Write a Personal Mission Statement

Your first step in creating a marketing plan should be sitting down with your journal and writing out a personal mission statement. Your mission statement doesn't have to be long or elaborate, it just needs to spell out your career objectives, your personal and professional goals, and your vision of how you want your life to look like - both short and long-term.

Additionally, your personal mission statement should answer the following two questions: *Exactly who am I, right now, as an employee or professional? And now that I've defined my career goals and objectives, what do I need to do to accomplish those objectives?* These are two fundamental questions that you should answer before proceeding with your marketing plan.

You should also identify some past success as part of your mission statement. Take some time to think back and pinpoint three or four personal successes you've had in recent years. These achievements could be work-related, or things you've accomplished at home or in your community. Write them down in your journal. Then see if you can find a common theme – or themes – in these examples. If so, these need to be part of your mission statement as well.

You should also identify some of your core values. These are the things you believe in, deep down inside. Write down a list of qualities that you think define you as a person, not just an employee. Some examples of core values could be working hard, being considerate to others, honesty, loyalty, creativity, etc. Also, your priorities in life should be aligned with your core values. When they're not, you're asking for trouble, and you risk ending up in a career (and life) that goes against your principles, and will leave you miserable in the long run.

Step #2: Develop A Unique Selling Proposition (USP)

So what exactly is a unique selling proposition, or USP? Basically, a USP is what makes you unique in the marketplace. It's your competitive advantage over the other job-seekers vying for your target occupation. What unique skills, talents, and abilities do you bring to the table? What attributes make you the best candidate for that open position? How will you make your future employer better as an organization? What sets you apart, and makes you a better option than all those other candidates?

One of the biggest mistakes that many job-seekers make is that they never find a way to stand out, and so they become just another name on a list, just another applicant among dozens or even hundreds of other applicants.

A strong USP can drastically improve your marketability and positioning with would-be employers. It gives them a reason to grant you an interview (and hopefully, hire you). A good personal USP should successfully answer this question: *What about my USP will jump out to a hiring manager, and cause them to consider me over the other applicants for his job?*

Creating an effective USP needn't be a tedious or time-consuming process. It can be as simple as identifying a couple of your qualities that are unique to you, and would make you singularly qualified to work in your target occupation. Perhaps you have a unique skill-set, or work experiences that would make you an outstanding employee. Or maybe you have professional traits, values, or aptitudes that you're proud of, and would make you an ideal fit for the position.

These are the qualities that make you exceptional at what you do, and are the foundation of your personal USP. They're the skills that you want to highlight to a potential employer. They're the things that you do better than anyone else at your current (or past) organization. Experience is the best teacher, and these are your hard-earned lessons from years on the job.

There are any number of personal traits you could use to develop your USP, and I won't try to cover them all here. But spend as much time as you need to on this exercise, and ask a close friend or family member for help if you need to. Always strive to make your USP memorable and remarkable in some way, and make it brief, clear and honest. Sell your personal brand, make it appealing, and stand out from the crowd.

Step #3: Create an Elevator Pitch

An elevator pitch, if you didn't know, is a concise summery of the problems you solve, how you solve them, why you enjoy solving them, and who you solve them for. It should convey your competitive advantages, and why you'd be the best candidate for the job. All this in a couple of short-but-effective sentences.

But your elevator pitch shouldn't read like an impersonal grocery list of your achievements, either. You don't want to sound like you're reciting your resume point for point. Many job-seekers are guilty of this, unfortunately, and their elevator pitch sounds about as compelling as reading the ingredients on a cereal box.

Instead, try making your pitch personal rather than professional. Instead of prattling off a list of accomplishments like a robot, try talking about your motivations, and why you love the work you do (or want to do). Forget that the other person is a recruiter or hiring agent for a moment, and communicate with them a one-to-one level. For example, your elevator pitch might sound something like this:

"My passion in life is sales. I love everything about the

process of selling products of value to people who can really use them. I'm a people person, and I enjoy connecting with people and finding out their needs, and how the products I sell can help fill those needs. I like the challenge of turning a skeptical stranger into an enthusiastic supporter. I've been in sales for over a decade, but I'm still learning new things every day, and I love using that knowledge to make myself better at my craft. I plan on being a successful salesperson for a long, long time."

The next step is to wrap all this together into an effective marketing plan. Your plan can be anything you want it to be. It's your life - and your job search - after all. But some of the areas might want to focus on in your plan include the following:

- **Building your own personal brand**. I'll go into this process in more detail in the next chapter, but having your own personal brand is a key component of an effective job-search marketing strategy.

- **Working on your people skills.** If you're not an extrovert who's at ease in social situation, you'll probably want to develop your skills in this area. Networking is vital to any successful job search, and you'll want to be good at meeting and befriending "influencers," and other people who can help you.

- **Building an online marketing platform**. If you have your own personal blog, that's great. But a blog isn't necessary to building your own marketing platform. Some of the social media sites like Facebook, LinkedIn and Twitter will work just as well. And chances are you're already using some of these services.

- **Establishing social credibility**. Social credibility means that people in your social network trust and respect you. They listen to what you say, and they think of you as an expert in your field. You especially want to build this level of credibility with potential employers, recruiters, and hiring managers.

Do these things, and you'll have a solid marketing plan that will put you miles ahead of the competition. But remember not to chisel your plan in stone. You'll want to adjust, and make modifications to your plan as circumstances in your job search change. You might decide to pursue a different career field, for example, or find part-time employment while you go back to school. This is a fluid and ever-changing process. But if you have a marketing plan - and you stick to that plan - you'll be well on your way to building a network and online presence that'll be hard for employers to ignore.

Chapter 3: Create Your Own Personal Brand

Creating a "brand" for yourself might seem like an unnecessary step when you're job searching, and you have so many other things on your plate as you weigh your employment options. But creating a professional brand is important for anyone who's looking to improve their career trajectory - even if they're currently employed in a job they love. And it's especially vital for job-seekers who are trying to stand out in a crowded and competitive job market.

Creating a strong personal brand - especially online - will highlight your skills and unique abilities, and will give recruiters and employers a strong first impression as they seek candidates for open positions. Think of your brand as your calling card, and make sure every aspect of your online presence portrays you as a top-notch professional who would be an asset for any organization.

Establishing a personal brand will let employers know that you're competent, reliable, and skilled in your profession. You'll come across as a worthy candidate that they'll feel comfortable investing in. After all, given the choice between two promising candidates - one with a strong professional online brand, and the other with a shoddy or non-existent brand - which one would you expect an employer to choose?

Positioning Yourself as an Online "Brand of One"

Most people think of branding as something that big companies do, companies like Coca Cola, Apple, and General Motors. And they're right. But individuals can engage in branding on a smaller scale as well, and set themselves apart from other job-seekers vying for the same openings.

Just for fun, try Googling your name and see what comes up. If you have a fairly common name, chances are you'll see a lot of people in the search results other than yourself. In fact, you may have to scroll through quite a few pages before you find your own LinkedIn or Facebook profile on Google – that's assuming you have a LinkedIn or Facebook profile to find.

Make no mistake, most recruiters and prospective employers will take the time to look you up before calling you in for an interview. Time is money for these people, and they'll want to learn as much about you online as they can before investing an hour or more in a face-to-face meeting. So you'll want to make sure what they see when they Google your name is positive, professional, and makes a good first impression.

In simple terms, your personal brand is your work history, professional skills, and life story as they appear online. So your online profiles need to be truthful and accurate, while at the same time presenting you as an attractive candidate to an employer or recruiter. Be someone that jumps out at them. Make yourself practically irresistible, so that your name is the first one they think of when they're looking to fill an open position.

So if you don't already have a LinkedIn profile, create one. This is the first place most employers will look when they want to scan your resume, and get an idea of who you are as a person and a prospective employee. You may already have Facebook and Twitter accounts, but you'll want to update those as well so that they reflect the professional image you're trying to present to the world. I'll go into these social media platforms in more detail later in this book.

Your brand needs to be memorable, and should reflect your education, skills, and qualifications. It should also highlight your expertise in a specific area. We live in an age of specialization - from doctors to football players to retailers and advertisers. Your situation is probably no different, and you need to position yourself as a specialist in a specific industry, trade or profession. We all become quite good at the things we do on a daily basis. Just about everyone is an expert at something, and you'll want let recruiters and employers know what you're good at (especially as it relates to your industry or career field).

We spoke in the previous chapter about identifying your competitive advantages as they relate to today's job market. These need to be reflected in your brand as well. If you have unique talents, or you bring special skills to the table, make sure that information appears in all of your social media profiles.

But be careful here. You don't want your online presentation to come across as pushy, self-centered, or too aggressive. There's a fine line between promoting yourself and beating your own chest, so you might want to have someone you trust look your profile over before you release it to the wider world.

Your Personal Branding Statement

You should also think about creating a short "branding statement" for yourself. In the previous chapter, we went through the process of developing a Unique Selling Proposition, or USP. If you took the time to develop a USP for yourself, then this will form the backbone of your branding statement. Your statement needn't be long – just 15 to 20 words is enough – but it should clearly state your competitive advantages in the marketplace. Why you're a unique employee, and why you'd be a perfect fit for that job opening in your field or industry.

Once you have a good branding statement in place, you should highlight it in all of your marketing materials - your resume and cover letter, your social media accounts, your blog or website (if you have one), your email signature, and anywhere else a recruiter or potential employer would see it. While this shouldn't be a canned message that you repeat over and over to everyone you meet, it should communicate your brand across all of your online profiles.

If you're stuck on this step, you could probably use the "elevator pitch" you created in the previous chapter. Just tailor it to fit your brand. Keep in mind that an employer mainly wants to know what you can do for them, so make sure that comes across in your branding statement. Also don't go overboard with the hype – present yourself as confident and authentic, not boisterous and overbearing.

Once you have a good branding statement, you'll want to start applying it to all of your job search activities. Think of it when you're trying to decide what profile photo to use on your social media accounts. Have it in mind as you step through the door of a job interview. Use it when you talk to a recruiter at a job fair, or when you're putting together your personal network. You want it to be the first thing people think of when they hear your name, both online and off.

Here are some additional tips and strategies for building your brand and ramping up your online presence:

Tip #1: Use your name effectively. One of the benefits of having a personal brand is that it helps to raise your profile and online search visibility. When recruiters and prospective employers search your name on Google, you want *your* profile to be the one that appears at the top of the listings, not someone else with the same name. Soyou're your name in as many places as possible, especially on all of the major social media platforms. Also see if you can register your name as a .com domain name. This might be difficult if you have a common name, but you could always add a job title like MBA or CNA at the end. Something like JohnDoeMFA.com is usually available for purchase on a domain site like Godaddy.com.

Tip #2: Use the same photo on all your profiles. Your photo is part of your image and personal brand. Be consistent with your online presence, and use the same profile photo on LinkedIn and the other career sites, plus your personal social media accounts including Facebook, Instagram and Twitter. Get rid of that goofy selfie you took on your last vacation, and replace it with a professional portrait with you dressed in business attire. That consistent image will help build your brand, and make you more recognizable to recruiters and prospective employers.

Tip #3: Create a video resume. If you're comfortable in front of the camera, then creating a video resume can be another way of building your brand and standing out in a crowded job market. Career websites like Vault.com and CareerBuilder.com currently offer hosting of video resumes. Keep the video brief and professional, make sure to include your branding statement in some form, and look it over carefully before posting it online. Remember that an online video can go viral, so you don't want to post something you'll regret later.

Tip #4: Use LinkedIn as your branding hub. Since most employers will go to your LinkedIn profile first when they're considering you as a candidate for a job opening, use the site as a jumping-off point for the rest of your online profiles. LinkedIn provides a "links" section where you can link out to your Facebook and Twitter accounts, your company website, your blog if you have one, and more. If you've invested a lot of time and energy into building your brand on these platforms, make sure potential employers can find them.

Tip #5: Keep your professional and personal lives separate. As I've mentioned before in this book, you'll want to make a good first impression if you intend to get that great new job in 2017. The last thing you want is a potential employer looking at your Facebook account and seeing a bunch of photos from your best friend's bachelor party - with half-naked strippers in the background. Or that post where you discussed the crude and inconsiderate behavior of your ex-boyfriend, in minute detail. We're all human, and it's okay to show your personal side to employers. Just keep it brief and in good taste when you can. Also remember the viral nature of the Internet before posting anything that could haunt you later.

Hopefully this gives you some good ideas about how to shape your brand and your personal image going forward. Personal branding is an ongoing project, and you should keep working on it even after you find that next job. How others view you will be important now, and well into the future, especially when it comes time to hand out the bonuses and promotions. So make sure your brand is aligned with how you want to be perceived, both inside and outside of your organization.

Chapter 4: Build A Personal Network

One of the keys to a successful job search is building and maintaining an effective professional network. I'm not talking about a list your drinking buddies, or your scrapbooking group, or your casual Twitter friends. My definition of a professional network is a list of people you know - either professionally or socially - who are in a position to help you find a new job. People with whom you share a common interest. People who are on the inside of the industry you're targeting, or better yet, people who work for a company you want to work for.

It has been estimated that over 60% of all jobs are found via networking. People finding jobs through the people they know, or relatives, or through the *friends* of people they know. So your ability to engage and develop your network from a variety of contacts - family, friends, association members, college alumni, current and former co-workers, people you meet at networking events, etc. - should be one of your top priorities going forward.

For many of the best job openings out there, the only way through the front door is by knowing someone on the inside. Someone who's in a position to help you, and who *wants* to help you. These are the gatekeepers, and the more of these people you know - at the companies where you want to work -

the greater your chances of landing that coveted job. As the old saying goes: it's not what you know, but *who* you know that really makes the difference.

Start Building Your Network

In order to build a large and effective network, you'll have to get out there and meet some new people, both online and off. You also need to be something of a shameless self-promoter. If this type of face-to-face schmoozing doesn't come easy for you, see if your spouse or an extroverted friend can accompany you to social and networking events. It often helps to have a wing man (or woman) along to offer moral support and help break the ice. But in the end you're going to have to be the one making the connection and nurturing the relationship.

There are two basic types of networking you can engage in. You can either dive in head-first and ask everyone you know to help you make new contacts and generate job leads. Or you can take a more indirect route, and form a sort of "mentoring" network where you solicit advice and general information to help in your job search. In either case, you'll need to hit the pavement - and go online - in order to contact as many people as you can. Again, this type of "cold calling" might be difficult if you're an introvert. But the meek probably *aren't* going to inherit the earth, and in most cases the "lone wolf" job-seeker has a rough time finding the best jobs. That's just a fact.

So suck it up and start building as large a network as you can. Open up your phone book and start making phone calls.

Attend as many networking events as you can. Join online chat groups and forums. Send out emails (but keep them brief and to the point. And watch that spelling and punctuation!). Attend career and job fairs in your area. Even parties and social events can be good places to add more quality people to your network. Just slip into the conversation that you're looking for a new job, and see where it goes.

Another good place to make contacts is at association meetings and events in your area. You'll usually find that many of the participants at these events share your goals and aspirations, and will gladly exchange business cards and contact information. Another idea is to volunteer to work at the event as a way of meeting more people.

Also, never think of people in your network as just names on a list. Think of them as your business partners. These are your friends, your inner circle of colleagues and confidantes. When you're in the market for a new job, the people in your network are the most important people in your life (outside of your family), and these are the folks who can supply job leads, offer critical advice, and introduce you to the right people inside your target employer.

Here are some additional tips for building a strong and effective professional network:

Tip #1: Start by taking an assessment of your current networking skills. Be brutally honest here. If you're an introvert who doesn't make friends easily, don't be ashamed to admit that to yourself. There are plenty of very successful introverts in the world, including entertainers, politicians, writers, business leaders, etc. In fact, most people aren't born schmoozers, but we all find ways of interacting with people and making friends. Just put your fears aside and get yourself out there. After all, what's more important, being safe and comfortable, or getting the results you want?

Tip #2: Sit down and list all of the people you know who could possibly help you in your job search. Leave out no one, even if at first glance they seem to be unlikely candidates. If you think they could be of assistance - either directly or indirectly - then write down their name. Sometimes help comes from the most unlikely places - like that plumber across the street who has an uncle who's an executive vice-president of the company you want to work for. Go all the way back to your high school days, and include high school and college classmates, teachers, members of your family, your current and former friends and co-workers, family friends, former employers, people you know from church, and anyone else you can think of.

Tip #3: Always look for ways to add more names to your network. Until you've been hired at your new job, you should regard this as an ongoing process, and keep adding quality people to your network at all times. The goal is to build a network that has both quality and quantity. Also realize that that you'll be scratching names off your list over time, so you'll need to add replacements to prevent your network from dwindling down to nothing. This is especially important if your networking list has less than 50 people. Look to build a network of at least 100 people, and 200 is even better.

Tip #4: Go after the "power players" in your field. The idea is to add as many high quality connections as you can to your network. These are the movers and shakers in your industry, and they can make a real difference in your job-search efforts. These should include established experts, upper-level managers, and people who make the hiring decisions at your target firms. Don't be concerned that you might never be in a position to meet these people, put them on the list anyway. Even if only five percent of these people every become part of your active network, you'll still be way ahead of the competition.

Tip #5: Make good use of online networking. Especially on popular sites like Facebook and LinkedIn. The idea is to leverage social networks to raise your visibility, promote your personal brand, and make contacts around the country (and even around the world). If you're not familiar with it, LinkedIn is the #1 networking site for professionals, and it's designed to help job-seekers and other people meet and connect on an open platform. The Internet is a powerful recruiting and networking tool, but be aware of where you're spending your time online. It's easy to get caught up in casual socializing, when you should be focusing on your job search network.

Tip #6: Don't be shy about asking your network for help, and always be willing to help them in return. Your network is intended to be a job-search tool, so don't be bashful about calling someone on your list and asking if they can help you in some way. If they're truly a friend or colleague, they'll be more than happy to oblige. And don't be one of those people who expects help from others, but never offers to return the favor. Let it be known that you're willing to provide any assistance you can to those in your network. Pay it forward, as they say, and good things will come back to you in spades.

And finally, don't get discouraged if you seem to be coming up short on your initial networking list. Lots of people lament the fact that they're not part of some "good old boy" or "good old girl" network. But those kind of networks are mostly fantasy in this day and age - at least for the majority of us. So keep it real, start with what you have, and build your network over time. Get creative. Meet and connect with people in your field whenever you can, any way you can, and you'll have a growing professional network before you know it.

Chapter 5: Update Your Resume

Having an updated and professional-looking resume is vital if you're searching for a new job in 2017. Everyone should review and update their resume at least once every six months, even if they're currently employed and not looking to make a career move. Situations change (and change without warning), and you don't want to be scrambling to update a resume that hasn't been looked at in years.

So be proactive, and make it a habit to update your resume anytime something significant changes. There are any number of situations that call for updating the information on your resume, including:

- You get a promotion
- Your role or duties change at your current organization
- You upgrade your education or training (new degrees, certifications, etc.).
- You receive a work-related award
- You help your employer to:

    Generate more revenue
    Attract more customers
    Save time & money
    Make your job more efficient

Solve a specific problem, or series of problems
Be a more competitive company
Expand your department, or the entire business

- You publish something important in your industry
- You move, or your contact information changes
- You've been laid off, or are currently unemployed for any reason.
- You hear rumblings of possible changes at your current employer (possible downsizing, company relocation, mergers, etc.).
- You're unhappy with your job, and looking for a career change

Keeping your resume current and ready for submission will give you a competitive advantage over your less-prepared competitors. Every little edge helps in today's job market, and having a well-crafted resume will allow you to meet with recruiters and hiring managers with confidence.

Here are ten tips for updating and polishing your resume:

Tip #1: Make sure your resume is focused. One of the mistakes that many job-seekers make is writing a resume that's too general, and lacks a clear focus. Hiring managers are very busy people, and they may only spend a few moments scanning your resume. So you need to highlight your unique skills and abilities, and make it crystal clear why you'd be the best candidate for that open position. Think about the branding statement you created in Chapter Three. Anything else should get pushed to the back of your resume – or be left out all together.

Tip #2: Make sure your name and contact information appears at the top of your resume, with your name in a slightly larger font. Also include your street address, your home phone number, yourself own, and your primary email address.

Tip #3: Feature your most important job-related skills in the top of your resume. Don't bury this information at the bottom, where the employer may never read it. Get those critical skills (assuming you have them) in the top one-third of your resume, where they'll stand out and get noticed by the people who matter.

Tip #4: Use bullet points in your resume. A bulleted style will make your resume more reader-friendly, and employers tend to prefer the use of bullets as this makes the document easier to scan. And be sure to use bullets consistently – don't use them in one part of your resume, then switch back to a straight-paragraph style in another section.

Tip #5: Begin at the end. Try not to overwhelm yourself by taking on your entire resume at one time. Break it up into "chunks," and start by looking at the bottom section of your resume to see if anything new should be included. Take into account things like recent promotions, awards, certificates or professional training, new degrees, etc.

Tip #6: Take a hard look at where you've been, and where you're going. The goals and aspirations you had when you first wrote your resume might be very different from what they are now. Take a careful look at each item on your resume, and ask yourself: *Is this really relevant to my current career goals?* If the answer is no, don't be afraid to re-word or even delete the item. Sometimes less is more, especially if the item doesn't apply to your current situation.

Tip #7: List out 3 to 4 key accomplishments for each of your work experiences. You'll also want to use bullet points and short sentences to describe each of those achievementss. Keep it short and to the point, then move onto the next accomplishment.

Tip #8: Update the look of your resume. Times have changed, and a resume that looks outdated and tired just won't cut it these days. So don't simply just add new information to that dog-eared resume of yours, give the entire document a facelift as well. Change the format to something current - either yourself, or through the services of a resume writing firm. Also make it available in multiple forms - Microsoft Word, a text-only file, and have it converted into PDF format as well.

Tip #9: Proofread your resume carefully, several times. Catch all the grammar, punctuation, and spelling mistakes that you can, then pass your resume off to someone you trust and have them look it over as well. Nothing will make you look more unprofessional to a prospective employer than having multiple mistakes on your resume. They'll assume you didn't care enough to produce a clean and professional document, so your attention to detail and quality of work probably aren't that good, either.

Tip #10: Print your resume on off-white paper. This might seem insignificant, but the paper stock you use for your resume can make a difference. Instead of white, try something modest but professional, like a cream, light blue, or green-tinted paper. This will help your resume stand out in a pile of white-paper resumes, and standing out is a good thing. In addition, a heavier, 20lb stock paper is generally the best to use for this purpose.

Finally, take your time and don't rush the process of drafting an up-to-date and professional-looking resume. This is a document that could very well make or break your job search efforts, so it's worth the time to make it as perfect as you can. And if you can't do the job yourself, don't be afraid to spend some money on a professional resume writing service. It would be well worth the expense if it leads to that great new job in 2017.

Chapter 6: Conduct an Effective Online Job Search

As noted in the Introduction, if you're searching for a new job in 2017, you're in luck for a variety of reasons. For one thing, the employment landscape is better right now than it's been since 2008, when the economy shed millions of jobs during the start of the Great Recession. There are also more quality job openings now than at any other time this decade. Another big advantage today is the ability to use the Internet, and especially social media, to reach many more employers than you ever could in person through an offline job search.

Today's job market is a completely different world from the one our parents experienced in their time. Technology has moved rapidly in the last twenty years, and the way people communicate, network, and go about finding jobs has changed just as quickly. Modern advances like the Internet, social media, online career websites, blogs, mobile apps, and other virtual tools allow job-seekers to scan thousands of quality job openings from the comfort of their home or office.

There are dozens if not hundreds of different career websites (also referred to as employment sites or job boards) to choose from, all designed to help people find the job or career they're looking for. These sites serve a dual purpose, as they also help recruiters and employers fill their job openings. This has made it easier than ever to find a job, anywhere in the country. And all the important information about that job is available as well, including geographical location, salary range, job duties, education and training requirements, necessary work experience, work schedules, and more.

But all of this data at your fingertips can also lead to information overload if you're not careful. You need to be selective, disciplined, and have a good online search strategy. Otherwise you risk spending all your time scanning job listings, and Twittering, and filling out countless online applications. With so many resources available, it's easy to fall into an unfocused job search that will leave your eyes red and your fingers sore, with little or nothing to show for it.

So the challenge is to come up with an effective online strategy. A strategy that will leverage your time, and allow you to contact as many potential employers as possible - employers with the job openings you're looking for.

Develop a Simple but Effective Plan

A simple online job-search strategy focuses on just a couple of the employment sites that are best-suited for the type of job you're looking for. That way you won't be creating profiles and submitting your resume to dozens of different sites, many of whom will be a waste of your time. Focusing on a handful of carefully chosen sites will usually be more productive, and save you time and effort that would be better spent elsewhere.

You also need to have realistic expectations going into an online job search. The Internet isn't a magic wand that will land you a high-paying job that you're not trained or qualified for. That six-figure executive position at an industry-leading company may sound great, but if you're not qualified for that position, don't waste your time applying for it. Decide what's realistic for someone with your credentials, education, and experience, and stay within those parameters for the best chance of hearing back on a job opening.

Working With the Major Job Search Websites

As mentioned earlier, the online career sites can be some of the most useful tool in your job-search arsenal. These sites give you access to thousands of employers in one place, employers who are actively seeking qualified candidates just like you. But keep in mind that some sites are better than others, and you don't want to waste your time on a site that's not likely to deliver the results you're looking for. The most effective career websites tend to be ones that provide the best connections, job leads, career advice, resume and interviewing tips, and more, all in one easy-to-use package.

Here are some of the important steps to take when using a job search website:

Step #1: Select the right sites (see Strategy #7 for more on this topic). Not all of the job search sites are the same, and some are tailored toward a specific industry or career field. Choose the sites that are best suited to your particular needs, and you'll increase your chances for success.

Step #2: Create your website account & profile. It goes without saying that you'll need to set up an account, and create a profile for each of the career websites you plan on using. Your personal profile is your "sales page" on the site, and it's where potential employers go to find out more about you. Your profile should include all of your relevant information, and should highlight your unique strengths and attributes as an employee. Remember your branding statement? Also, make sure to include important keywords in your profile, so recruiters and hiring managers will have an easier time finding you.

Step #3: Search for job vacancies that interest you. Most of the big employment websites have powerful search engines that allow you to scan hundreds or even thousands of open positions. You can filter your search by geographic area, salary range, education and experience requirements, etc.

Step #4: Once you comb through the listings on a particular site, and you identify a shortlist of potential employers, check out what else the site has to offer in the way of career guidance, networking groups, resume databases, and more.

Step #5: Activate job alerts. Almost all of the major career sites have a job alert feature, and this is one of the more useful tools for locating promising job openings. Simply go into your profile and turn on the appropriate alerts, and you'll be notified when job vacancies meeting your criteria become available. The alerts can either be sent directly to your profile page, or to your email address, whichever works best for you. Personally I prefer the email option, as I can check my inbox and see alerts from several different job sites all at once.

Step #6: Start building an online network (see Strategy #4). Having the ability to build a professional online network – especially on the social media sites like Twitter, LinkedIn and Facebook - is a vital to your job-search success. Many of the bigger career sites also offer networking groups, and these can be great for connecting with fellow job-seekers, recruiters, and other important people in your target industry.

Step #7: Use JibberJobber. The JibberJobber service is a powerful tool that allows you to track exactly where you've sent your resume, and what jobs you've applied for. It lets you organize and monitor your networking contacts as well. This is an especially valuable service if you're working with more than four or five job-search sites at the same time.

Step #8: Be professional in your communications with networking and other job-related contacts. This isn't the time or place to mess around - save that for the golf course, or the beer pub. When conducting a job search, all of your emails and other correspondence should businesslike and professional. Keep it short and to-the-point, and be sure to proofread everything *twice* before hitting the "send" button. There are few things worse than sending an employer an email full of typos and grammatical errors.

Step #9: Keep track of where you've applied, where you've created a profile, and where you've posted your resume. You'll also want to keep a record of all your passwords (never use the same one, unless you want an identity thief raiding your accounts). One idea is to create an Excel spreadsheet where you can keep record the name of the website or job board, passwords, when you applied, etc.

Utilizing Career Blogs in Your Job Search

Job and career blogs are different from the employment websites like Monster.com or CareerBuilder.com. Blogs are typically smaller, geared toward a narrower topic or niche, and the best ones are loaded with valuable job-search tips and information. Blogs serve as a sort of online career advisor, with guidance and insights you're not likely to find on the big job board sites.

What you won't find on most career blogs are things like job listings, or a way to create a profile and post your resume. They also don't normally offer a way for you to contact a recruiter or employer directly. Blogs are more of a personal "web log," or online journal, and they offer encouragement, advice, and insight into the trials and tribulations that most job-seekers face on a daily basis.

Blogs are also interactive in that most of them allow you to leave comments after a post or article. You can offer your own take on the topic, add additional information, give the post a thumbs-up or thumbs-down, or add a friendly hello. It can be comforting to connect with other job-seekers from all over the country, and know that you're not alone in this sometimes-lonely and often frustrating task of finding a new job.

Most blogs offer an RSS feed that you can subscribe to. This allows you to see any new posts or other content added to that blog without visiting it directly. You can even aggregate several feeds onto a dedicated RSS reader like FeedDemon. That way you can scan all your feeds in one place, and pick out the posts that interest you. This can be a real time saver, especially when you have so many other job-search tasks vying for your attention.

One challenge with job and career-related blogs is the fact that there are hundreds and hundreds of them on the Web. So the task becomes finding a few that you like, and are best suited to your needs. You might start by doing a Google search for blogs dedicated to your target industry, then find a couple of general career blogs on topics like personal branding, networking, interviewing, or writing effective resumes and cover letters. Then follow those blogs for a few weeks to see if they provide the information and community you're looking for.

Here are some additional tips for choosing good career blogs:

Tip #1: A blog should have a specific purpose. Whether it covers a wide range of career-related themes, or it only focuses on a narrow topic like networking, a good blog should always have a clear intention. If you spend a few minutes scanning a blog and you can't figure out what its purpose is, you should probably move on to the next one. Some blogs are designed merely to generate advertising revenue from the search engines, and aren't concerned with helping the visitor at all.

Also, some of the best career blogs are "developmental" blogs. These are intended to offer information and advice to help people grow in a specific area. Some examples would be personal or career development blogs, entrepreneurial development, spiritual development, etc.

Tip #2: A blog should look and feel professional. It should have a clean, professional design, and not look like something that was cobbled together over a weekend. It should have well-written blog posts and articles, with good titles and professional quality photos. Avoid blogs that use crude language, offer politically-incorrect commentary, or have lots of typos and other grammatical errors in the writing.

Tip #3: A good blog is well organized and easy to navigate. The blog should have a simple, easy-to-understand layout without a lot of unnecessary links, pop-up ads, and flashing banners. Nothing annoys me more than when an ad pops up while I'm trying to read a blog post. Or a blog where I can't figure out how to find previous posts on the topic I'm most interested in.

Make it Easy for Employers to Find You

This last piece of advice may sound obvious, but you'd be surprised at how many job- seekers devote hours and hours to an online job search, then make it difficult for employers to even find them. And even if you're not actively seeking a job right now, by making your online profiles up-to-date and easy to find, you might get an unexpected job offer that's too good to pass up.

Insuring that your resume and credentials are easily accessible online should be a top priority. You may not realize it, but many recruiters and hiring managers actively seek out "passive" job candidates to help fill their open positions. These are qualified candidates that may or may not be in the labor pool, but who might be interested if the right offer came along. Almost everyone could potentially fit into this category, as the "make me an offer I can't refuse" saying rings true for most people.

One way to raise your visibility is by registering with the major online job boards, even the ones you haven't submitting job applications or resumes to. Headhunters and hiring managers regularly scan these job portals for promising candidates, so make sure you have a presence there. You'll want to create a profile on career networking sites and blogs, college alumni associations, employer alumni associations (which include many of your current and former co-workers) and any professional associations you belong to.

There are also candidate sourcing programs like Airs Sourcepoint that many companies use to help fill their vacant positions. So make sure your resume is out there where these recruiters can find it, and you'll significantly increase your chances of landing that new job.

And don't forget keywords. If you want your resume to be found by a lot of people, make sure it's loaded with searchable keywords. All of the major search engines use keywords to help index and catalog the information in their databases, so you need to know which keywords employers would use to find you. If you're not sure which keywords to target, try visiting a career search engine like Indeed.com and search for jobs that are a fit for your skills and qualifications. Look at the job descriptions carefully, and identify words that important to that industry. Once you've identified some terms that apply to you, make sure to include them in your resume, job application, and online profile.

So there you have it. By creating an effective online marketing strategy - and learning how to use the best career websites and blogs - you'll be able to spend your time more productively. You'll cover more ground in less time, you'll get your name and profile out there in front of as many potential employers as possible, and you'll give yourself the best chance of being successful in your search.

Chapter 7: Focus On The Top Career Sites

As mentioned in the previous chapter, one of the pitfalls of today's inter-connected world is the fact that there's so much information out there. They call it the information super highway for a reason, and if you're not familiar with the job-search landscape, you can easily become lost and confused amid the hundreds of career websites and blogs, job boards, informational videos and podcasts, recruitment and employment services, Facebook and Yahoo! groups, and more.

You're much better off choosing a handful of sites that match your job-search requirements, and then focus exclusively on them. Tune out the noise and online distractions, and spend you precious time on the activities that will bring you the most results. But also don't be in too much of a hurry to decide which sites and job boards to use. Each site has a slightly different take on the subject, along with its own audience of job-seekers, and of course employers who troll the site looking for promising candidates. So take your time, and make sure the sites you choose are a good match for you and the industry you work in.

The online job boards and career search engines can distribute your resume to hundreds of companies and employment centers with the click of a mouse. The downside of this is fact that on the large career portholes like CareerBuilder.com and Monster.com, it's easy to get lost among thousands of competing job-seekers. This is where the action is, and so these big sites attract the largest audience on both sides of the job-search equation.

Many times you'll have a better chance of being noticed on one of the smaller, industry-specific employment sites. This is also why you should run a narrow, focused job search as opposed to going too wide, or becoming too general with your search criteria. If you work in the healthcare field, for example, seek out sites and job boards that focus specifically on nursing and other medical jobs. If you work in the automotive industry, narrow your search to sites that specialize in that area.

Things to Look For in a Career Website or Job Board

You might be wondering what the difference is between job search engines and a job boards. The job search engines typically aggregate job listings from multiple job boards and employer websites, and make them available in one place. Whereas a job board is a catalog of job openings posted by individual employers. One major advantage of the job search engines is the fact that you can run advanced searches, and filter out the results by location, education and qualification requirements, starting salary, job duties, work schedule, and more.

So you should take this into account as start filtering through the online resources available to you as a job seeker. Do your homework, run industry-related Google searches, and ask your friends on social media. Search for sites that seem like a good match for the type of job you're looking for.

The following are some criteria to help you filter out the best sites:

1. Does the site seem active, and does it have a lot of listings?

Needless to say, an employment site that's the virtual equivalent of a ghost town isn't going to be much help in your job search. You want sites that are loaded with recruiters and employers who are looking for candidates just like you. So look for active sites that seem to have lots of registered users and current job listings. If you're not sure about a site, ask on social media and see if you can find out what kind of experiences other job-seekers have had using that service.

Also double-check to make sure the job listings are current. Some employment sites have trouble attracting a wide enough audience to stay relevant, and so their listings are sparse and outdated. Look at a sample of listings and check the posting dates. If all the listings are undated, or most of them seem to have been listed that day, then this is usually a tipoff that something is wrong. With an active site, you should see listings with a wide range of posting dates, with new ones been added on a regular basis.

2. Does the site seem easy to use?

Career websites and job boards should be user-friendly, and easy to navigate and use. If you can't quite figure out where to go on the site, or how to register and submit your resume, or where to find the job listings you're interested in, it might be time to move on. Websites are supposed to make your job search easier, not harder. So don't waste your time on a site that you're not comfortable using, no matter how highly-rated and popular it is.

3. Do you have to pay to access job opportunities?

Generally, as a job-seeker you should never have to pay to gain access to current job listings. The standard practice is for the recruiter or employer to pay the fees on their end in order to be listed on the site. So if you're being asked for your credit card information right up front, you should immediately move onto the next site on your list. (Note - there are some "executive" sites that do charge an up-front user fee, so take that into consideration if you're seeking an executive-level job. Just try to get some assurances as to the quality of the opportunities you'll have access to. Look for executive sites that offer a money-back guarantee, and (verified) testimonials from satisfied clients).

4. If it's an industry-specific site, does it have type of jobs you're looking for?

The site needs to have current listings in your industry, in your target income range, and in your geographic location. It goes without saying that it's a waste of time to apply for jobs in a different, unrelated field, or halfway around the world (unless you're willing to relocate there). Often the name of the site will be a good indicator (like WeldingJobs.net or NursingCareers.com), but not always. Get good at screening sites quickly, and pass on ones that don't meet your criteria.

5. Is it easy to post your resume, and will you be able to edit it later?

Registering on an employment website, and posting your resume, should be a straightforward and painless process. It should be no harder than adding your resume to a networking site like LinkedIn. It should also be easy to edit and update your resume (or delete it) later, as circumstances change. If it looks difficult (or impossible) to make these changes, it might be a good idea to pass on the site and apply your efforts elsewhere.

Beware of Scam Career Websites

Unfortunately, in these days of malicious hackers and cyber-security, you need to be aware that there are scam sites out there. These fraudulent job sites are looking to take your money, or capture your personal information so they can resell it to bad actors on the Internet. These websites might look real enough, but they're completely fake, and their only purpose it to lure you in with bogus job listings that sound really good, and entice you to fill out a resume, or submit your credit card information.

These sites prey on people's desire (or need) to find a good paying job or career, and the "work from home" industry is especially rife with these types of scams. And once the bad guys have your personal info, it's usually too late to get it back. So if you're searching on the Web, and you come across a suspicious-looking career site or job board that's not listed in section below, be very cautious before giving them any of your important information.

Here are a few tips for screening employment sites for safety and security:

Tip #1: Google it. Run the website's name through Google and see what comes up. Google's the world's largest search engine, so take notice if they seem to have little or no information about the site in question, or if the information they do have is mostly negative. If that's the case, pack up and move on as quickly as you can.

Tip #2: Check for site ownership. Any legit career site or job board will have a "about us" or "contact" page that lists the owners of the site, including a business name and street address, and an active phone number. The next step is to run the company name through Google (and the Better Business Bureau website) to see if it's an actual company, and if there have been any complaints lodged against it. Never use one of the smaller or lesser-known employment sites if you can't verify ownership.

Tip #3: Check the site's privacy policy. The next step is to look over the site's privacy policy (and if you can't find one, then scratch the site off your list and move on). The privacy policy should clearly state what data the site collects, and how it uses that information. Pay particular attention to how they handle the information on your resume. Some sites will sell your contact info (phone numbers, email addresses, etc) to third-party companies, when then use it to bombard you with unsolicited promotions and advertising.

Tip #4: Check for seals of approval. You've probably seen these verification seals on various websites. These are seals from organizations like the Better Business Bureau, Truste, Thawte Site Seal, and others. Make sure the site you're considering has at least one of these displayed on its home page. Also make sure you can click on the seal - if you can't click through to the verification site, and check that the seal is current and in good standing, then scratch that site off your list.

Finally, if you have any doubts about a career website or job board, take a pass and move on. It's not worth the risk to your personal information. You can also visit the Federal Trade Commission's "Jobs & Making Money" page at http://www.consumer.ftc.gov/topics/jobs-making-money for more information on this topic.

A List of Some of the Top Job Search Websites & Blogs

Now that you know what to look for employment websites and blogs, here's a list of some of the top sites currently on the Internet. Be aware that things change quickly online, and a top website today could be an also-ran (or even gone) tomorrow. But the following sites are all large, well-established platforms, and should serve you well as you hunt for that great new job in

2017.

Monster.com – You've probably already heard of Monster.com. This company does a lot of advertising, and they're one of the most popular career and job-search websites. Setting up a profile and posting your resume is easy, and you'll have your choice of thousands of current job listings in just about every industry and career field you can think of.

Indeed.com - Indeed is regarded by many as the top online job website. Indeed aggregates job information from hundreds of different career sites, blogs, trade associations, classified ads, etc. and makes them available in one place. You'll find literally millions of job listings here. In addition to being able to post your resume on Indeed, you'll also have access to lively discussion forums, and a wide variety of job search tips and advice, company research, and more.

CareerBuilder.com - is a combination job search engine/career information site with loads of articles, and other tips and advice for job-seekers. CareerBuilder also has tens of thousands of current job listings pulled directly from employers, online classifieds, job boards and newspapers.

LinkUp.com - LinkUp is another big player in the job search game. A job search engine, LinkUp offers job listings directly from thousands of company websites. The postings are current, and are updated daily from large, mid-sized, and smaller company job listings. Some of these postings are unadvertised, and you won't find them anywhere else, so make sure LinkUp is on your short list of job-search resources.

Vault.com - Vault is a career information porthole. The site provides career advice and job listings, plus a wide variety of information including employee surveys of top employers, industry-specific career guides, advice articles and much more.

USAjobs.gov - USAjobs is the Federal government's official job listing website. The site has thousands of government job listings, plus employment search, a general information center, veteran-specific information, a variety of printable forms, and more.

Dice.com - If you're an IT or other tech job-seeker, Dice.com is a great place to search for job openings. You can run advanced searches by job title, employer, starting salary, geographical location, and other keywords. The site is easy to use, and you can upload your resume and start tracking jobs right away. Dice also has a free career advice and tech news section for job seekers in this industry.

Careerealism.com - This blog was built on the theory that all jobs are temporary. The site has a wealth of career advice articles, and tips on interviewing, resume building, handling a layoff, personal career development, and more. Careerealism also has a robust set of job-search tools that are free to use.

TheDailyMuse.com - The Daily Muse is part blog, part job-search tool. It's a valuable site for both job-seekers and employers, and the content is organized into sections for career advice, job search, career paths, management, entrepreneurship, and more. This is also a good place to find inspiration beyond the usual interview and resume tips.

This is admittedly an incomplete list of the top career websites and blogs. There are many more out there, especially if you're looking for niche employment sites that cater to a particular field or industry. Some of these industry-specific sites can be quite valuable to your job search, so they're worth going looking for. There are usually fewer competing job-seekers on these sites, and all the job postings will be in your target industry.

Chapter 8: Use LinkedIn To Connect With Recruiters & Employers

In case you're not familiar with LinkedIn, it's a social networking site designed for professionals and other job-seekers. The site is a very useful platform for just about every working person and student, no matter what their field or area of study. LinkedIn is an enormous database containing millions of resumes and profiles from all over the US and abroad. It's a powerful networking tool, and thousands of people every year find a new job on this platform.

Unfortunately, LinkedIn isn't very user friendly, and you'll have to spend some time learning its quirks and features before you'll feel comfortable posting your resume and networking on the site. You'll also want to stay active and engaged on LinkedIn if you expect to get the maximum job-search benefits. If all you do is occasionally update your profile, then sit back and wait for recruiters and employers to reach out to you, you might be less than satisfied with the results.

How Linkedin Works

If you're a professional, you're probably already familiar LinkedIn. If not, just know that LinkedIn is a popular social site that helps both professionals and non-professionals connect and network with one another. To join LinkedIn, you simply go on to the site, open a free account, and then create a profile. The basic LinkedIn profile consists of a profile headline, a resume section, and your history and business interests.

If used correctly, LinkedIn can be one of the most effective tools in your job-search arsenal. The site (unlike many of the other social platforms like Facebook or Instagram) is designed for business, and LinkedIn is a great place to meet and interact with recruiters, potential employers, current and past co-workers, former classmates, and more. Adding contacts to your LinkedIn account allows you to associate with important people in your industry, and lets your contacts to keep up with you as well.

Another great feature of LinkedIn is the ability to view the contacts of people you've already connected with. Then when you locate someone you think could be helpful in your job search, you can ask one of your contacts to arrange an introduction. Your network will begin to grow, and with luck you'll eventually contact people who make the hiring decisions at the companies you're targeting.

Note - one thing you'll need to be careful of is approaching people you don't know on LinkedIn. The folks at LinkedIn tend to be very sensitive about how people meet and interact on their site, and they don't want spammers blasting out sales messages and mass emailings. If you send out too many unsolicited requests to connect with strangers, and those requests are denied or reported (i.e. the person doesn't know you, and doesn't want to know you), then LinkedIn may ban you from adding new contacts in the future. In a worst-case scenario, your LinkedIn profile might even be deleted. So when reaching out to people on LinkedIn, make sure it's someone you know, or you have some sort of context around why you're contacting that person.

Searching for People on LinkedIn

A good place to start your job search efforts on LinkedIn is by using the site's powerful search capabilities. LinkedIn allows you to run advanced searches for people based on several factors: name, job title, location, company or organization, professional status, background, etc. Then, when you locate someone of interest, you can view that person's contacts to see if any of them are connected to you.

Try searching for former co-workers, classmates, or previous bosses and supervisors. Also search for industry leaders whom you don't already know. This is also why it's important to use the proper keywords in *your* profile. Search is a two-way street, and many recruiters and employers find promising candidates by scanning profiles and resumes on LinkedIn. With the ability to search for keywords in an individual's headline and profile, hiring managers are able to contact job-seekers from anywhere in the country - or anywhere in the world, for that matter.

If you set up your profile correctly - and you use the important keywords in your industry - you have a great chance of receiving unsolicited emails from recruiters and employers who are interested in hiring you. So do your homework, and take the time to set up a search-friendly profile so you'll be easy to find on the site.

Make Your Headline Count

Another important feature of your LinkedIn account is your profile headline, which appears just below your name. You need to think of your headline as your personal branding statement, because your name and headline are often the only thing a recruiter looks at when scanning the site for promising candidates. If the headline doesn't interest them, they won't even click through to view the rest of your profile.

You only have a moment to make a good first impression, so your headline and your profile picture need to be professional and appealing, and they need to stand out from the crowd. If you don't have good current photo of yourself, consider paying a portrait photographer to take one. And never try to use one of your school portraits for this - especially if it's more than a few years old.

As for your headline, you'll want to use power words that will intrigue the reader, and entice them to click through to your profile to read more. This is the same principle that newspapers and websites use to attract readers to their news stories and articles. So look for ways to highlight your skills in your headline, while at the same time standing out from the crowd. So instead of writing a bland headline like "IT Software Professional," you might try something more intriguing like

"Skilled IT Professional Looking To Make A Difference."

Think of your headline as sort of an "elevator pitch" that sums up your unique qualifications in a single sentence. If you're stuck for ideas on how to write a good headline, you might spend a few hours scanning headlines on LinkedIn to see what others in your industry are doing. See what jumps out at you, and what leaves you cold. Imagine that you're a headhunter or recruiter, and note which headlines you find most appealing. Then model your own headline around that same format.

Note - another factor in how you write your headline is whether or not your job search is "out of the closet" or not. For example, if you're unemployed - or you don't care that your current employer knows you're looking at other options - you can be a lot more open and aggressive with your headline. You could write something like "Experienced IT Professional Actively Seeking Opportunities."

However, if you *don't* want your current employer to know that you're searching for a new job, you'll want to be a little more discrete with your headline. You won't able to send signals to recruiters that say "I'm available, give me a call!" But you can still generate interest by making sure your headline is original, appealing, and reflects your skills, passions, and experience.

Target Specific Companies, and Follow Them

Once you've completed your profile on LinkedIn, you'll want to start putting together a "target list" of specific companies that meet your search criteria. Then, with a list of promising candidates in hand, you can begin to follow those companies via their official LinkedIn pages.

This gives you a window into these organizations, and is an invaluable way of finding out what they're currently doing, and what they have planned for the future. Once you start following a company, you'll be notified when that company announces anything new or interesting. It could be news about their future hiring plans, or perhaps the company is opening a new branch office in your area, or they just inked a big new government contract. Many times you can learn this information before it's released to the general public, and get a leg up on the competition.

Using Linkedin Groups in your job search

LinkedIn groups are another great way to increase your visibility on the site, and can lead to all kinds of employment opportunities. These professional groups are really just another networking opportunity, and there are groups built around almost any topic you can think of. Search for groups that are related to your field, industry, or area of expertise. You'll find groups on LinkedIn for real estate agents, healthcare workers, IT professionals, lawyers, accountants, plumbers, construction workers, etc. And if you're not able to find a group related to your professional area, you can always create your own.

In order to take full advantage of LinkedIn groups, consider the following strategies:

- Join in the discussion. Group discussions are a wonderful opportunity to showcase your knowledge and talents in your area of expertise. Another plus is that recent discussions are displayed on the group home page, and are also sent out in notification emails to every user in that group. Also, when you find someone in the group you want to connect with, respond to their discussion posts as a way of breaking the ice and adding them to your network.

- Another way to get noticed in a group is to post news items that are relevant to the group topic. Become a "newsmaster" within the group, providing valuable industry insight, relevant news items, and other information as a way of becoming a thought leader in the group.

- Sometimes job openings are posted in groups, so be on the lookout for these as well. Many people found their current job after seeing it listed in a LinkedIn group.

Creating your own group can also be a very valuable. As the group creator, you'll have extra visibility, and the opportunity to connect with everyone who joins your group. You'll be viewed as a leader, and someone who has a lot of credibility in your industry and career field.

Be Sure To Stay Active on LinkedIn

One of the keys to success in marketing yourself on LinkedIn - and anywhere else for that matter - is to remain active and "top of mind." As with any of the social media platforms, if you neglect your account for weeks (or months) at a time, you'll quickly lose relevance and visibility, and your networking effectiveness will suffer as a result.

Simply joining LinkedIn and posting your resume isn't enough. You need to stay active and engaged in order to see real results in your networking efforts, especially with so many others competing for the same jobs. Continuous and sustained activity will ensure that you remain visible on the site, you'll be someone who is looked to for current information, and this can lead to many unsolicited job opportunities in the future.

And don't think that you'll need to spend hours a day staying active on the site. Many people can do everything they need to do on LinkedIn in fifteen or twenty minutes.

Here are a few more reasons to stay active on LinkedIn:

- When you're active and engaged, you show up in LinkedIn's activity reports, which are in turn emailed out to your contacts and connections. This helps to ensure that you remain top-of-mind within your network.

- Your name is included in group emails - which again increases your visibility within the group.

- You will continually show up on the profiles of those people that you interact with - which in turn increases your reach.

Here are some activities that will help keep you engaged on LinkedIn:

- Answer questions, show your in-depth knowledge of the subject.

- Update your profile on a regular basis. Even if everything is current, you could always tweak your headline, or add more important keywords to your resume.

- Post fresh content to one of the LinkedIn groups.

- Add connections. You should always be looking for new people to add to your contact list.

- Recommend a friend or coworker on LinkedIn. Pay it forward, and your helpfulness will eventually be rewarded.

These are just a few suggestions for sustaining your relevance on LinkedIn. Remember, the larger your network, the more visible you will be to recruiters and employers, and the more new job opportunities you'll have going forward.

Chapter 9: Use Facebook To Find A New Job

I've long been aware of the value of using LinkedIn for professional networking, but I was surprised to learn recently that Facebook is the most popular social media site when it comes to finding a new job. By far. According to one recent survey, almost 19 million Americans found their current job on Facebook, which is more than LinkedIn and Twitter combined.

Most people don't think of Facebook as a job-search tool, but it can be if used correctly. With almost 1.5 billion registered users worldwide, Facebook has more members than all of the other social media sites put together. Which means you'll potentially have more reach on Facebook, and more visibility with recruiters and employers searching for qualified candidates in your industry. For that reason alone, Facebook is worth tapping into as you look to build your professional job-search network.

As you probably know (because you're probably already a member), Facebook is a social platform that allows you to connect with people you know – i.e. friends, family, co-workers, former classmates, etc. The site also allows you to post photos and videos, share your profile, update your status, post news about family and friends, brag about your recent vacation to Europe, play games, follow your favorite brands or companies, and a whole lot more.

Facebook is all about connections. But it works a slightly different than LinkedIn, where you can search for people based on keywords in their profile, or their company name. Facebook doesn't allow this type of broad searching – you have to know who you're trying to connect with - or be a member of a group or network - before you can make contact. For this reason, it you'll have to use a slightly different strategy when it comes to building a professional network.

Facebook Job-Search Strategies

Just about everyone has a profile on Facebook at this point, so I won't go into detail about how the site works or how to set up an account. If you need help in this regard, you can visit the site and view tutorials on how to join and set up your profile.

As far as using the site as part of your job search efforts, I've included some steps that might help you as you build your network and get yourself "out there" on Facebook:

Step #1: Add your professional history to your profile.

In addition to listing your favorite books, movies, and TV shows, Facebook provides an easy way to add your work experience and credentials as well. Just find the "update info," button near the top of your profile page. Then click the "Work and Education" link along the left column. Facebook provides slots where you can list your current job and position, along with descriptions of your education, skills, accomplishments, and other work-related details.

If you want to make yourself visible to the thousands of recruiters who scan Facebook looking for job candidates, you'll want to fill this section of your profile out carefully. Just as with LinkedIn, you'll want to make sure you include important keywords that recruiters would use when searching for qualified candidates. To save time, you can even cut and paste much of the information out of your LinkedIn profile and use it on Facebook.

Step #2 - Classify your friends and start a professional community on Facebook.

The idea here is to separate your professional contacts from your casual friends and family, so you can customize your message for each group. If you have hundreds of friends on Facebook, this might seem like a labor-intensive task, and it certainly can be. But you'll find that it's well worth the effort if you intend on using Facebook effectively in your job search.

Anyway, to classify people on Facebook, go to the section where your friends are listed. Move your cursor over the "friends" box next to the name of one of your professional contacts. You'll be shown a number of lists, including an option to create a new list. You'll want to create a new list titled "professional."

The next step is to scan through all your friends and identify the ones whom you would consider professional or work-related contacts, then add them to your professional list. This will allow you to target and communicate with those people separate from your everyday friends and family. That way you won't be sending your professional contacts pictures of your best friend's bachelor party, or your weekend getaway to Cancun.

While it's a good idea to humanize yourself by occasionally sharing bits of your personal life with your professional contacts, you'll want to stick to business most of the time. Facebook also allows you to filter out sections of your content, so that it's only visible to specific groups. For example, when you're ready to post a status update that's intended for your friends and family, click on the "Public" icon that's just left of the word "Post." You'll see a menu with the option "Custom." Click on that, and then on the "Don't share this with," where you'll want to type "Professional."

Step #3 - Start networking and making connections.

The power of social media is its ability to connect you with like-minded people who have similar interests and backgrounds. Networking is essential to finding a good job in 2017, so take every opportunity to meet new people expand your list of contacts. Facebook and LinkedIn share some common features, and both offer powerful networking opportunities. But Facebook allows you to connect with people you may know personally, rather than professionally, and these are the people who often become your most valuable resources during a job search.

One way to start this networking process is by typing the name of a potential employer into the Facebook search bar. Then click your cursor in the search bar a second time and you'll see a pulldown menu that includes "My friends who work at ___ company." If you click through that tab you'll be shown all of your Facebook friends who work at the company in question. Then, under those people, you'll see another option box with the words "Friends of my friends who work at _____ company."

This is where you can really kick your networking efforts into high gear. Even though you don't know these folks directly, you can still send out a friend request via Facebook. If you're really lucky, you'll connect with someone who can recommend you for an open position at that company. Otherwise it's a matter of getting the word out that you're interested in working for the firm, and letting your network spread that message for you.

Step #4 - Join and become active in Facebook groups

Groups are one of Facebook's most powerful features, and you'll find many opportunities to meet and interact with people in groups, people who can potentially help you in your job-search efforts.

Groups on Facebook are very similar to LinkedIn groups, in

that they're a place to post news and information about a particular topic, industry or career field. And just as with LinkedIn, you'll want to add value to a Facebook group by jumping in and contributing to the discussion. Show off your hard-earned knowledge and expertise, and be relentlessly helpful. In addition, if want to get involved on a deeper level, you can volunteer to moderate or manage sections of the group as well.

As with all social media, the key to networking on Facebook is active engagement. You can't just join a group, never contribute anything worthwhile to the conversation, and then sit back and expect the job offers to come rolling in. It could happen, but don't hold your breath. You're much better off being proactive, and reaching out to like-minded individuals wherever you can. Show people what you know, share information (including your opinions, as long as they're not offensive), and be helpful and outgoing.

Once you've had a few conversations with someone in a group, then you can go ahead and send them a friend invitation, and they're likely to accept. You especially want to reach out to people who are "players" in your industry, and who have networks of their own. The more friends the better, and this could lead to you being considered when job openings become available, even before they're advertised to the general public.

Step #5 - Post valuable content, and respond to others

It's always a great idea to find information that would be valuable to people in your network, and then share it on

Facebook. Things like industry news and trends, links to quality websites and blogs, information about your company's accomplishments, media interviews, insider tips and tricks, and anything else what would be helpful to your online friends. Become known as a valuable resource within your group, and people will begin to think of you as *the* expert in your field.

Also pay attention to what your professional contacts are posting. Make it a point to "like" their posts, and offer intelligent comments as well. When you help others, they'll want to help you in return, and again this could lead to a job opportunity that you might not be expecting.

You'll also want to post the occasional personal item, such as important news about your family, or an exciting trip that you're planning. This is a way of humanizing yourself within your network, and letting people know a little about your personal life. Just keep these posts brief and occasional, and don't share anything that you'd be embarrassed to tell your boss, or a hiring manager during a job interview.

Step #6 – Explore the Facebook Marketplace

Facebook Marketplace is similar to Craigslist in that it allows you to create a personal listing for just about anything - including your desire to find new employment. Your listing will go out to your friends, professional network, and even other networks on Facebook.

Companies and recruiters also post job listings in Marketplace, so you'll want to spend time every day scanning those as well. These Marketplace job listings are hit-or-miss, but you'll occasionally find something worthwhile, and you'll be able to see a short description and also who posted the job. Then you can apply directly, or get in contact with the person who posted the opening for more information.

Facebook's marketplace may not be as comprehensive as other marketplaces, but that can be an advantage, as you'll likely face less competition from others in your industry.

In conclusion, Facebook can be a valuable resource if used correctly, and millions of job- seekers have used it to build their professional network and locate open positions. If you're not already using Facebook in this manner, you should seriously consider jumping on board. The size of the site alone makes it a great opportunity to make your next job search a short and fruitful one.

Chapter 10: Using Twitter As A Job Search Tool

The third social media platform I'd like to discuss is Twitter. You're probably already familiar with Twitter, as it's the second-largest social media platform with more than 640 million registered users. You may have even used Twitter for job-hunting in the past. According to one recent survey, over eight million Americans report that they found their current job through Twitter, which is third behind only Facebook and LinkedIn.

But Twitter is different from those other social media sites in several ways. First off, Twitter is a "microblogging" platform, where your posts are limited to 140 characters or less. Which means you have to be direct and to the point with your communications. On Twitter you don't have space to ramble, or beat around the bush, and this microblogging format is ideal for job-seekers who don't have a lot of time to devote to a social media campaign.

Another major difference is that unlike LinkedIn or Facebook, you can reach out and connect with anyone on Twitter, whether you know them or not. This makes it easy to add dozens or even hundreds of followers in a short amount of time, without sending out unsolicited emails or other tactics that can get you banned on those other sites. And this freedom to connect with thought leaders and power players in your industry can be a big advantage if used correctly.

Twitter's openness also makes it an easy place to showcase your personality, interests, skills and talents. Headhunters and recruiters can read through your tweets and get an idea of who you are, how you think and operate, and whether or not you'd be a good fit for their company. Twitter allows you to tweet back, send private messages, and develop a rapport with people you might not have access to offline.

The format on Twitter also encourages a quicker response from recruiters. Something that's tweeted travels around in the world in seconds, and it's easier and more convenient for a recruiter to reply to your tweet than to call you on the phone. The platform also allows private messaging, although again you're limited to 140 characters or less.

Setting Up Your Profile on Twitter

As mentioned several times in this book, it's essential for job-seekers to make a positive first impression on social media. Recruiters and employers are busy people, and they often scan hundreds of profiles at a time before choosing two or three that interest them.

So your first order of business is to set up a professional profile on Twitter, with a username, description, and photo that stand out from the crowd. You want to look accomplished, but interesting at the same time. Unlike LinkedIn and Facebook, you don't have the room to add your resume and other work-related information on your Twitter profile. They only provide space for a short bio, your location, and a website address. So every word has to count. You'll also want to include links to your Facebook and LinkedIn profiles, so recruiters can access your full history and resume if they feel you're a promising candidate.

To maximize your chances of being found by a potential employer, you'll want take your time, and weigh every element of your Twitter profile very carefully. The following are some items you'll want to consider as you're setting up your profile:

Your Twitter Username

This might seem like a no-brainer, but you need to put some thought into the username you choose on Twitter. You have the option of either using your real name, your profession, or your personal "brand" as your username. Also keep in mind that your username forms the basis of your Twitter URL (or web address), and this will be visible in any links to your profile.

Again, aim to be professional and memorable. Avoid trendy or cutesy sounding usernames if you plan on leveraging your account as a job-search tool. This is another area where you don't have much space to work - Twitter only allows a total of 15 letters and numbers in this field. Blank spaces aren't allowed, but you can add underscores to separate words, numbers and letters.

You might also consider adding a professional designation to your name, if you have one. These are job-related and relevant keywords like [name]CPA, [name]MBA, etc. Just make sure the title is appropriate, accurate, and relevant. This little touch can be valuable in your job search, as it helps to broadcast what you do, and your qualifications to do it.

Your Twitter Account Name

This is separate from your username on Twitter. Your account name is your "handle" on the site, and it's another chance to add important keywords to your profile, and distinguish yourself from the competition. When someone views your profile page on Twitter, they typically see your name, followed by the account name just beneath it (the @yourname or @yourbusinessname). This field is 20 characters long, and you can add spaces and punctuation marks in addition to numbers and letters in your account name.

Your account name also forms the second half of your Twitter page URL. This is the title at the very top of the browser window. This is what you'll use when you want to create a link to your profile from your blog, your website, or another social media account. By inserting your important keywords into your account name, you'll also help Google and the other search engines send traffic to your profile via keyword-rich Web searches.

If you're like most of us, and you have a common name that might be used by hundreds or even thousands of other people, you can differentiate yourself by adding your middle initial to your account name. This is also an additional way of branding yourself. If you do add your middle name or initial, be sure use that exact same name on LinkedIn and Facebook, so recruiters and employers will be able to find you there as well.

Your Geographical Location

When using Twitter as a job-search tool, you'll also want to include your geographical location, so recruiters will know where you live and work. They often use location keywords when searching Twitter for job candidates. And if you're planning on moving to a new location in the near future, and you'll be seeking a job there, you can use that location in your profile in place of your current address.

The Rest Of Your Profile

Your Twitter bio is another place to distinguish yourself, and attract attention to the fact that you're a quality candidate seeking employment. Every character of real estate on Twitter is important, and you'll want to write a bio that says a lot in just a few carefully-selected words. You only have 160 characters available in this field, so you'll have to choose the most important items from your resume to include here.

It's also important to add your target keywords (again) into your bio, while at the same time writing sentences that are readable, and make sense. Try to imagine what keywords an employer in your industry would use to search for candidates like you. You might also add the URL for your LinkedIn profile here as well, so interested parties can go there and read your entire resume.

Two examples of effective Twitter bios might look something like this:

Network Admin Specialist w/10 years experience in configuration of Cisco in a LAN/WAN, Wireless and IP telephony environments. Looking for a position in the NYC area.

Recent college grad, engineering major, seeking an entry-level engineering position on the West Coast. Have intern experience at a Midwest utility co. Available for immediate employment.

The last items in your profile are your photo and a link to your blog or website. Make sure your photo looks professional - you don't want a selfie from your trip to Sea World here. Dress up and pay a professional portrait photographer if you have to. Another idea is to use your LinkedIn profile photo in your Twitter account for consistency, and to reassure employers that you're the same person.

How to Network Effectively on Twitter

Networking on Twitter isn't that different from networking on Facebook or LinkedIn, the main differences being the openness of the platform and the character limits on your tweets.

Here are a few additional tips for building a solid job search network on Twitter:

Tip #1: Follow leaders in your target industry. Find companies and individuals in your industry or career field, and follow them. Many companies today have job-related Twitter handles, and following them will keep you updated on current job openings. Also listen to what these companies and individuals have to say on Twitter. Track emerging trends and industry news, and soak up as much relevant information as you can. And look for the prominent recruiters in your industry, and start following them as well.

Tip #2: Build a solid and reliable network. Your network on Twitter - and the other social media sites – can become your #1 job-search asset, so treat it that way. Most recruiters realize that if they hire you, they'll inherit your network as well, so don't abandon it after you get hired. Focus on connecting with quality people, and building a solid network, both inside and outside of your industry. Join Twitter groups. Interact and start conversations. Reach out to people who motivate and inspire you. And don't be afraid to step out of your comfort zone once and a while.

Tip #3: Be helpful and supportive. This is good advice no matter what you're doing. The idea is to enhance your reputation, and build friends and allies on Twitter by reaching out and helping others. If you help and support other people in your industry, they'll do the same for you, and it won't be long before an employer takes notice. Also, don't think of Twitter only as a platform for self-promotion - show a genuine interest in what others are doing, and tweet about their stuff before you tweet about your own.

Tip #4: Show your personal side. You don't want to be overly serious and professional on Twitter, even as a job-seeker. The short posting format on the site makes it a great place to cut loose and show your personality (just don't go overboard, and keep it in good taste). Allow recruiters a window into your character, and let them see your family, your interests, and the things you're passionate about. Employers are people too, after all, and they respond positively to candidates who display their human side once and awhile.

Tweeting Your Way To A New Job

Now we come to the core of using Twitter: tweeting. Also known as micro-blogging. The 140 character format on Twitter forces you to adopt a slightly different strategy when it comes to job-searching and networking on this platform. You won't be able to write a long essay on a topic that interests you, or offer a laundry list of your experiences and qualifications. On the other hand, composing an effective tweet should only take a few minutes of your time, and it could potentially reach a wide audience if it gets picked up and re-tweeted by a number of influential people.

Your tweets should demonstrate your knowledge of the topic, and show your willingness to share valuable information with your followers. They should also showcase your research and writing skills, and your ability to communicate complex ideas in a just a few well-chosen words.

Just as with LinkedIn and Facebook, you should try to position yourself as a source of recent, unique, and relevant information about your industry or career field (or both). Be a resource. Scour the Internet in search of the freshest tips and information to share with your followers. Link to valuable articles and blog posts. Subscribe to news RSS feeds and email newsletters, and follow them closely. Become known as one of the best sources of information in your niche, and you'll soon find yourself with an appreciative audience that is eager to help you in return.

Here are some additional tips on how to tweet effectively:

- When you come across a positive news item about a prospective employer, make sure to tweet about it. Also include the company's Twitter handle in the @companyname format, so they'll see it in their message stream.

- Re-tweet worthy content. When you come across a tweet that you like - or you think your followers would like - re-tweet it. Also RT positive tweets by people working for your target employers, or about a prospective employer.

- Stay on topic with your tweets. Employers don't care about the weather in your area, or that great cappuccino you got at Starbucks, or what's happening to your favorite team in the playoffs. It's okay to show some personality, but don't clutter up your professional feed with casual or useless banter.

- If you're including a link in your tweet, be sure to use a URL shortening service like Bitly.com or TinyURL.com to shorten long URLs. With only 140 characters to work with, you don't have the room to waste on a long URL link.

In summary, Twitter should be an important part of your social networking and job-search strategy going forward. And if you update and maintain your profile over time, you'll find that your Twitter account can be a helpful asset even after you've found that next job. Recruiters and employers are always searching for good people, so your account can become a major building-block for your career - both now, and well into the future.

Chapter 11: Market Yourself Offline

Okay, I've discussed several online job search strategies in this book. But if you want to go the extra mile – and you're really serious about finding that great new job in 2017 - you'll want to have an effective offline strategy at well. The Internet is great, and it's opened up a whole new world of possibilities for job-seekers. But you'll still need to get out and search "the old fashioned way" if you want the best chance of landing a new job this year.

One problem with an online-only job search is the fact that it's easy to become lost in a sea of fellow job-seekers. It has been estimated that over 450,000 resumes are posted on Monster.com every week, and Indeed.com gets over 100 million visitors per month. That's a lot of people competing for a limited number of job openings.

So improve your odds by spending at least some of your time job-searching offline. Many people think that hunting for a job offline means picking up the phone and cold-calling potential employers in your city or town. But there are easier and more effective ways of contacting recruiters and employers, including job fairs, One-Stop Career Centers, employment agencies, networking functions, and more.

Also, don't discount people you meet as you go about your daily business. That woman behind you in the Starbucks line could be a hiring manager at a local firm. Or your accountant might have a client who could use your services. Everyone knows somebody, and it pays to meet and engage with as many people as possible as a way of building and maintaining your network.

Attend Job Fairs in Your Area

If you're serious about finding a new job - and using every means necessary in order to realize that goal – then you should consider attending at least one job fair in the city or town in which you live. Job fairs might seem intimidating at first - sort of like an employment supermarket, with probing eyes looking at you from all directions. But having so many potential employers all under one roof can be a huge advantage. A job fair can save you a lot of time and legwork in your job search, and fairs needn't be scary as long as you come prepared, and you're committed to making the experience work for you.

Thousands of people find gainful employment at job fairs every year. Employers are there because they have job openings they need to fill, and they need to find quality people to fill those positions. You'll be able to speak to recruiters, hiring managers, and company reps face-to-face, and on-the-spot interviews are not uncommon.

Job fairs are wonderful places to gather information about a prospective employer. Most companies in attendance will have reps on hand to distribute brochures and answer questions, and this can save a lot of time when you're trying to decide which jobs to apply for. The recruiters will also accept your resume, and even schedule an interview if they feel you're a good candidate for the position.

A fair is also a terrific way to "get out there" and get your feet wet in the job-search process, especially if you've been on the sidelines for a while. Because there are so many other job-seekers at fairs, it can seem less intimidating than showing up alone for a formal interview. A fair can ease you into things, and allow you to browse the booths and gather information on employers while you're deciding which ones to target. Attending a job fair can even be fun and exciting, and you can mingle and meet other job-seekers who are in the same boat you're in.

Just make sure you treat your time at a job fair seriously, and get everything out of it that you can. With their "one-stop shopping" format, fairs are wonderful opportunities to contact recruiters and employers - in a relaxed, informal setting – and can give your resume and application added weight with these people.

Here are some additional tips for making the most of any fair:

Tip #1: Treat it like a job interview. You should prepare for the job fair as if you were going to a formal interview, which means dressing appropriately, bringing an updated resume and cover letter. You'll also want to be polite at all times, professional, and try to build rapport with recruiters and hiring managers. Also be prepared to answer job interview questions on the spot.

Tip #2: Go to the job fair alone. Think of it as a business function (which it is), and leave your family at home. You don't want to be looking after your kids while you're trying to speak to recruiters. And if you insist on bringing a friend, split up at least part of the time so you don't appear to be an inseparable pair. The idea is to project a smart, professional image, and that's easier to do when you're alone.

Tip #3 - Survey the landscape and formulate a strategy. See if you can contact the fair organizer a few days before the event and get a list of participating companies. Then go through and rank the ones who interest you the most. Also try to arrive at the fair right when it opens, and take a walk around to get a feel for the layout and spot booths that look promising. Then plan a route that will allow you to visit your target companies in order, and avoid wasting time and wandering aimlessly around the building. It's also a good idea to save your visits to the most promising prospects for later, after you've had time to warm up at a few booths first.

Tip #4 - Take more than one application, and complete them flawlessly. When a company is handing out application forms at their booth, take two instead of one, and fill them out when you get home. Use the first application as a rough draft, so if you make a mistake you can discard it. Then use the second copy as a final draft to send back to the employer. And make sure to include a note mentioning that you met the recruiter or hiring manager at the fair.

Tip #5 – Treat every contact as a mini-interview. Every time you speak with a prospective employer, regardless of how briefly, you should consider it as a mini-job interview. Recruiters are at the fair to evaluate you, and they'll expect you to approach them and introduce yourself, be polite and professional, look them in the eye as you're answering questions, etc. Just like you would during a formal job interview.

Tip #6 – Learn as much as you can about the company. Job fairs are great opportunities to discover more about an organization, things you might not learn by visiting their website or Facebook page. Ask about their hiring process, and what jobs are available for workers with your skills and experience. And before you leave the booth, always make sure to ask for the recruiter's business card.

Tip #7 – Be organized, and take notes. The typical fairgoer is inundated with brochures, business cards, applications, and other literature. So bring along a briefcase or portfolio, or even a canvas bag, in which to collect and organize these materials. Also take notes while you're at the fair. There's a lot going on at these events, and it's easy to forget things, or have conversations run together in your mind. So take a small notebook and jot things down, then review your notes when you get home.

Attending a quality job fair is definitely worth the time and effort. If you've never been to a fair, or you don't know how to find one, there are a number of resources available to help you. Try checking with your state and local governments, career and trade associations, and employment centers for information on upcoming fairs in your area. The employment section of your local newspaper is another place to look, along with online job boards and Internet job fair locators.

Using a One-Stop Career Center

If you're not familiar with One-Stop Career Centers, then you're missing a great job-search opportunity. There are hundreds of these OSCC facilities around the country, serving almost every major population center. As the name implies, these centers are employment clearinghouses that provide everything a job-seeker needs under one roof. One-Stop Career Centers provide services for both workers and employers, and they offer a wide variety of training, employment, career counseling, education, and job search resources and training.

If you can't locate one of these centers in your area, you can often access one via computer or remote kiosk. But try to visit one in person if you can, as the staff there can meet with you and assess your skills and abilities, then help match you with potential employers. They can also help steer you toward any additional education or training you might need, and they even have consumer report information available on local schools and education providers.

When you visit an OSCC for the first time, you'll be given a registration form to fill out. There's no charge for signing up, and there are programs available for the disabled and ex-offenders. Once you've submitted your application, you'll be assigned an advisor who will work with you to determine your qualifications, and your career interests going forward. You may then be assigned to a career specialist, unemployment professional, or case manager, depending on your needs.

If you're new to the workforce, or you've been unemployed for an extended period of time, the folks at a One-Stop Career Center will help you develop the skills necessary to enter the labor market. They also have computer terminals available where you can perform job search and labor market research, look at available job listings, and also prepare your cover letter and resume. They also schedule interviews with employers if you qualify for an open position.

If you need to complete your GED, they can assist you with that as well. You can also use one of these centers to brush up on your computer skills, find out about colleges and trade schools in your area, and learn about opportunities for occupational and job training. You might even qualify for a scholarship or grant to help finance your continuing education.

To learn more about One-Stop Career Centers you can visit the Department of Labor Website at:

http://www.dol.gov/dol/topic/training/onestop.htm

Consider hiring a career coach or employment service

Employing the services of a career coach or counselor may be another a good option for finding work in 2017. If you've never considered using a career coach to help develop and further your career, you should consider it. I'm a career coach myself, and I've helped many clients identify the work they were born to do, and find jobs that match their passions, talents, skills and core values.

You should think of a career coach the same way a professional athlete thinks of an athletic coach or trainer. Even the best athletes need good coaching in order to reach their full potential. They need someone to instruct them, encourage them, listen to them, and push them to compete at their highest level. A skilled coach knows how to push all the right buttons, and help people perform better than they've ever performed before.

I've witnessed firsthand the value of having a professional guide to help navigate the sometimes-rocky road to finding a new job. Having someone in your corner who understands what you want, what you're going through, and who can offer objective and timely advice, is invaluable. Sure you can do it on your own, but you'll almost certainly have a better experience with the guidance and encouragement of a good career coach.

So what exactly should you expect after hiring a career coach? Expanded direction and self-awareness, for one. Career options that you probably never considered, for another. A coach will also help you clarify your job-search goals and objectives, so you'll know exactly what you want out of a new career, and where to get it. And if a coach helps you land that dream job, you can expect an overall improvement in your quality of life as well.

So how do you find a quality career coach?

Look online, for starters. There are several directories of professional career coaches on the Internet. Look for coaches who are certified by at least one of the professional organizations serving this industry. Some of the better coaches will also have additional certifications, and even advanced degrees in some cases.

Also be aware that this is a very personal process, and you'll need to feel comfortable with your choice of a coach. After all, this person can potentially have a major impact on your career – and your life as well. For the relationship to work, you'll need to feel comfortable with your coach, and be willing to tell him or her your career dreams and aspirations. For their part, the coach should be thoughtful and understanding, and offer moral support as well as objective career advice.

The pros and cons of an employment agency

Another option is to hire the services of an employment agency. Some people have had mixed results with employment agencies, but they can be a worthwhile investment if they help you find that new job you really want. They can also open up employment doors that you'd have a hard time prying open on your own.

Have you ever wondered why you can't seem to find any of those fantastic jobs that you read about on the big online job boards? It's probably because the employers with those openings are using an agency to fill them. These days, a lot of firms are looking to cut costs and outsource where they can, and so they're turning to employment agencies to do their initial candidate screenings and interviews. This saves the company the time and expense of wading through hundreds of resumes on their own, and then interviewing dozens of applicants just to fill one or two openings.

Even though employment agencies work both sides of the fence, that doesn't mean they don't have your best interests in mind. They assist job-seekers in a number of ways, including coaching, interview preparation, and even serving as their agent when it comes time to negotiate salary and benefits with an employer. Most agencies will also help you put together a winning resume and cover letter, which can be worth the commission fee all by itself. The agency is also available to answer general questions, introduce you to recruiters and hiring agents, and they'll even help if you have problems with your placement.

Just be aware that all this comes with a fee. Some people look down on employment agencies, mainly because of the commission fees they charge. But considering the agency can get you access to unadvertised job openings, and also help in your preparation and placement, the commission can be a small price to pay. Also keep in mind that sometimes the employer picks up the tab for your agency fees, so you might get lucky and get their services for free.

Chapter 12: Ace The Interview

Okay, you've made it this far, and you've (hopefully) gone through all the steps of creating a marketing plan, building a personal brand and network, updating your resume, and promoting yourself online and offline. With luck you'll get a quick and positive response, and you'll be invited in for that all-important job interview. Congratulations. You're in the game, and that great new job is within reach. But you'll still need to put your best foot forward, and make a good impression during the interview. Otherwise all your time and effort could be for naught.

A job interview is your chance to shine. The pressure's on, and what you say and do during those ten to fifteen minutes in the interviewer's office can either move you into the next round of consideration, or knock you out the door. But there's no reason to panic. With the careful planning and preparation, there's no reason you can't knock your interview out of the park, and be well on your way to that new job.

With that in mind, I've assembled a few steps that can help you get ready for your interview. Take these steps seriously, especially if you've been out of the labor pool for a while, or you're a recent graduate with little interview experience.

Step #1 - Do your homework on the employer beforehand

One way to make a good impression, and stand out during a job interview, is by knowing a lot about your prospective employer. And not just information that you pulled off their corporate Facebook page, but detailed knowledge about who the employer is, where they came from, what they do, and how they do it.

These days, employers expect job-seekers to be informed, and know a lot about the company, and why they want to work there. You may have done some initial research on the company before you send them your resume, but now it's time to dig deeper and learn a lot more about them. Don't skimp on this step. Interviews for quality jobs are hard to come by, and you need to make every effort to maximize your chances of making a good impression.

One of your first tasks while doing research is to discover what the employer's actual needs are, and how you are ideally suited to help them meet those needs. Remember your branding statement, and your competitive advantages. By learning what the employer's needs are before the interview - and how you can help them - you'll impress the interviewer with your preparation and attention to detail. Get this right, and you'll be well on your way to the next round of consideration, and a possible follow-up interview as well.

So what's the best way to research a prospective company, and uncover their needs when it comes to new employees? Fortunately, most of this groundwork can be done online. So open up your laptop and do some investigating on the following resources:

The employer's website – This should be your first stop when doing research on prospective companies. Start by clicking on the "About Us" button and see what comes up. Usually you'll get an overview of the company's history, what services and products they offer, how they view themselves, etc. Then go to the "News" section of the website for press releases and other current news and information. This can be a great place to search for an organization's needs. Study and think about the long-term implications of these news items. For example, will the company be expanding (and needing more employees), will they be exploring new markets, will they be securing government contracts and need more specialized workers, etc.

Social Media – this should be your second stop when doing employer research. These days most companies have profiles on social sites like Facebook, Twitter, LinkedIn, YouTube, etc. In fact many organizations have an entire marketing team devoted to maintaining their social media accounts. So visit these sites and see what you can learn about your prospective employer. Many times news and information will be more current on social media, and you'll also be able to see how the public interacts with the company, especially current and former employees.

Third party resources – you can often find a wealth of information about a prospective employer on third-party sites like Yahoo! Finance, GlobeInvester.com and MSNBC.com. Also check the big employment sites like Monster.com and CareerFinder.com for detailed financial, employment, and other company information.

Your offline contacts – these are people in and out of your professional network, who may have some inside information about a prospective employer. Ask around, and see if you know anyone (or one of your *friends* knows someone) who works - or used to work - at your target employer. If so, find out what they think about the company, what it's like to work there, and what are your chances of working there yourself.

Step #2: Dress the part

Make no mistake, you'll be judged on your appearance the moment you step through the interviewer's door. More than one job-seeker has done everything right as far as their resume and preparation for the interview, only to fall out of consideration due to their appearance. They say you can't judge a book by its cover, but all too often that's exactly what recruiters and hiring managers do when they're evaluating prospective employees.

If you're a man, you should always wear a business suit to a job interview, even if you're interviewing for a blue-collar position. But also try to match your suit to the type of job you're seeking. For example, if you're interviewing for a professional or "button down" occupation, you shouldn't wear a casual suit to the interview. And don't overdress if you're applying for a job as a tradesman or shift worker.

If you're a woman, you'll typically want to wear an plain dress to the interview – although a pantsuit is also acceptable. It's always better to be conservative than flashy in your appearance. You're not going on a date here, and you don't want to show up at an interview wearing a lot of glitzy jewelry or other accessories.

Also, make sure your clothes are clean and in good condition. This might seem obvious, but you'd be surprised at how many job-seekers show up to an interview with stains on their pants, or a snag in their panty hose. Your choice of shoes is important as well. For men, wing tips are a good choice, or even dress loafers if they're well-made and in good condition. Women should avoid open-toed and very high-heeled shoes, and leave the sandals and sneakers at home (unless you're applying for a job as a professional tennis player).

Step #3: Practice, Practice

Just like professional actors, singers, and athletes spend hours practicing and preparing for their big moment, you'll also need to set aside some time to get ready for that critical job interview. There's nothing worse than walking into an interview and being surprised by something, or fumbling to answer questions that you didn't rehearse ahead of time.

For starters, go over your research notes on the employer (refer to Step #1 above). You don't need to memorize everything about the company, but you should at least be able to explain what the firm does, and how they do it. Also go over your research on the company's needs, and how you're well-suited to meet those needs both now, and into the future.

The next step is to go over your resume. You'll want to know your resume by heart, and be able to give detailed explanations of everything that's on it. I'm always amazed at how many job-seekers neglect this step, and then they stumble when the interviewer asks them to elaborate on a resume detail. You should know all of the employment dates and company names, exactly what your job duties were, and how you contributed to the success of the organizations in question. And you should be able to recite these facts with confidence and authority.

Another good exercise is to sit down in a quiet place and spend a few minutes visualizing your upcoming interview. Close your eyes and visualize yourself walking through the door, greeting the interviewer with a firm handshake, sitting down and answering his or her questions. See yourself proceeding through the interview with relaxed confidence, and then finally getting up and leaving with the knowledge that you made a good impression on your prospective employer.

For an even more realistic practice session, you could elicit someone (preferably not a close family member) to participate in a mock interview. Give them a list of questions you're likely to be asked, plus few of their own that you're not expecting. If you own (or have access to) a video camera, then record the interview so you can review it later. Study your tone of voice, body language, eye contact, and how relaxed or nervous you appear. While this can be a little unnerving at first, you'll soon start to feel comfortable in front of the camera, and your confidence and comfort level will grow accordingly.

As far as rehearsing all the questions that could be asked during a job interview, the range of possible questions is almost endless, and is beyond the scope of this book. There are any number of good books published on the general topic of job interviews, along with industry-specific books and websites.

Step #4: Building rapport during the interview

Building rapport with the interviewer is important if you want to stand out from the competition. Don't be intimidated by the person on the other side of the desk. Always remember that the interviewer is a person just like you, and they've been in the same position that you're in now, at some point in their career. It's their job to assess not only your skills and qualifications as a potential employee, but also whether your personality and temperament would be a good fit for the position as well. That's why it's so important to build rapport with the person asking the questions.

Rapport begins the moment you walk through the door. Try to relax and be yourself right from the start, and always let the interviewer take the lead and set the tone. Be ready to offer your hand in a handshake, but only if the interviewer offers his or her hand first. Also try to match the tone and rate of speech of the interviewer. That is, if he or she speaks slowly and softly, you should too, without being too obvious about it.

It's also a good idea to show some of your personality during an interview, but don't go overboard with it. You're not "shooting the breeze," or catching up with an old friend from high school here. Never try to get too familiar with an interviewer, especially right off the bat. But it's okay to relax, smile when appropriate, and show your sense of humor. Take your cues from the other person, and observe whether or not they're matching your relaxed demeanor. If not, keep it straight and professional.

Body language and eye contact are also important. Look the interviewer in the eye as you're answering his or her questions, but don't stare back like an owl, either. Blink occasionally, glance around the room, use facial expressions when appropriate. Speak as if you were conversing with a parent, or another person of authority. Your body language should reflect a relaxed, alert, confident and enthusiastic job-seeker. Also avoid too much gesturing or fidgeting with your hands. When in doubt, keep your hands relaxed and resting casually in your lap.

Keep your responses short and to the point. Don't ramble, or try to make things up as you go along. And telling the interviewer more than he or she needs to know is usually a big mistake. Always use appropriate language during an interview, and leave out the slang and crude references, as they're likely to offend the interviewer and quickly bounce you out of contention for the job.

And finally, make an effort to listen carefully during the interview. This can be difficult if you're nervous and worried about making a good impression, but nothing turns an interviewer off more than an applicant who doesn't seem to be paying attention. So nod your head, respond in kind, and let the interviewer know you're listening and absorbing every word they're telling you.

Step #5: Follow Up After the Interview

This is an easy step that sabotages a lot of job-seekers. You can do everything right during the interview process, and make a great impression, but you still need to follow up if you want to maximize your chances of landing that new job.

Start by sending the interviewer a short thank-you note. This message serves two purposes. First it lets the employer know that you appreciate the time and effort they invested in you, and secondly it pulls you back into their mind and reinforces their (hopefully) good impression of you. This thank-you note also gives you a chance to include anything that you may have failed to mention during the interview. Don't go overboard here - just a couple of short sentences explaining a key point or two will do.

And instead of a handwritten note, be professional and print it out on a computer. It's also a good idea to send a short note of thanks to anyone at the company who was involved in your interview process. This sort of extra touch is something that most job-seekers neglect to do, and it can help set you apart in a crowded and competitive job market.

Conclusion

So there you have it. If you learn and act on the strategies in this book, you should be well ahead of the game when it comes to finding a great new job in 2017. As mentioned in the Introduction, this should be a very good year in the U.S. labor market, with thousands of jobs opening up each month. And not just minimum wage retail or restaurant jobs, but also good-paying salaried positions, as the economy grows and companies in every sector diversify and expand their operations.

But you should also brace yourself for the ups and downs of a job search. Even in a good economy, you're likely to face a lot of rejection out there. You'll need a healthy dose of confidence - and a positive attitude - as you search for that ideal new job. Try not to take the rejection personally - it's just part of the hiring process in a competitive and ever-changing business environment.

If you go through an exhaustive job search, but there just don't seem to be any jobs in your current field, it might to time to consider a career change. This can be a frightening prospect for many people - the idea of resetting your career from the beginning, going back to school to earn a second degree, and disrupting your work (and life) schedule can be scary for any number of reasons.

119

But don't let fear stop you from making a much-needed career change. Also take a look at parallel industries, or similar careers where it might be possible to utilize your current skills and talents. Take an aptitude test to find occupations that you might be unaware of, and that would match-up with your current qualifications. While any change in careers will probably require some degree of additional education or training, the process might be quicker and easier than you think.

You also need to think of your job search as your full-time job (especially if you're currently unemployed), and attack it every day. Plan your work, and work your plan. Get the little details right, and don't be afraid to go the extra mile. Do the things other job-seekers aren't doing. If finding a new job that's exciting and rewarding is really that important to you, then you'll find the drive and energy to exceed expectations at every turn.

Set your sights high, don't settle for something that's not worthy of your time and talents, and you'll be well on your way toward new career success.

Good luck!

About the Author

Don Allen is an author, blogger, and certified career coach. Don enjoys helping people be more productive, find satisfying careers, and become more successful at work and in business. Don is also a serial entrepreneur, and has own almost a dozen businesses over the past twenty-five years. When he's not coaching or writing, he's probably out hiking, kayaking, gardening or traveling.

Read Don's career blog at www.CareerCrossings.net

See Don's other titles at www.Career-Books.net

CPSIA information can be obtained
at www.ICGtesting.com
Printed in the USA
LVHW080050081218
599728LV00010B/79/P